Michael A. Rascona

A Hacker Never has a Bad Lie
True Golf Stories

Outskirts Press, Inc.
Denver, Colorado

This is a work of fiction. The events and characters described herein are imaginary and are not intended to refer to specific places or living persons. The opinions expressed in this manuscript are solely the opinions of the author and do not represent the opinions or thoughts of the publisher. The author has represented and warranted full ownership and/or legal right to publish all the materials in this book.

A Hacker Never has a Bad Lie!
True Golf Stories
All Rights Reserved.
Copyright © 2009 Michael A. Rascona
Illustrated by Bobbi Switzer
V1.0 R1.0

Cover Photo and illustrations © 2009 Outskirts Press, Inc. All rights reserved - used with permission.

This book may not be reproduced, transmitted, or stored in whole or in part by any means, including graphic, electronic, or mechanical without the express written consent of the publisher except in the case of brief quotations embodied in critical articles and reviews.

Outskirts Press, Inc.
http://www.outskirtspress.com

ISBN: 978-1-4327-2797-0

Outskirts Press and the "OP" logo are trademarks belonging to Outskirts Press, Inc.

PRINTED IN THE UNITED STATES OF AMERICA

Table of Contents

A Hacker Never has a Bad Lie 1
3-Iron to the Skull 3
Albatross wears a Toupee 7
Almost Perfect Shot 10
Arizona Fiasco 13
Blind Date 17
Buddy, Can you Spare a Club? 20
Ducks, Kittens and the Picture Perfect Shot 23
El Guappo 27
Follow the Bouncing Ball 29
Four Wedge Challenge 32
Go to Gull Haven 37
Have a Shot 43
He Stole my Putter! 45
I Never Liked that Club 47
It's a "Gimme" 49
Keep your eyes on the road… 53
Lady in Pink 55
Larry's Trick Shot 57
Perfection 59
Putters Beware! 61
Scramble and the Hedge 65
Shoeless Ed Shakes his Head 69
So, you want to be a Caddy? 73
The Big Miss 77
The Gadget Man 81

Up, Up and…Away? 83
Whady'a shoot? 87
Who Needs Friends Anyway! 89
Wildlife 93
Wolf 95

A Hacker Never has a Bad Lie

I hope you enjoy this compilation of true golf stories written by a certified hacker for those of us who play just a little differently from those making a living on the tour.

Sure, we all know someone with a hole-in-one on their golf resume. You've probably heard their telling of that shot a thousand times! You also probably know someone who holed an approach shot from 150 yards. It was no doubt spectacular, but certainly not unheard of. And how about those miraculous putts from 60 feet? You've seen it and perhaps credit yourself with one or two. Drives that might even impress John Daly are wonderful to watch and brag about, but they are witnessed by hackers every day of the week. Accounts of golfers with questionable skill and uncanny luck abound, so why celebrate the common place victories on the golf course when we can laugh at each other's follies?

Although I have never had a member of my foursome ace a hole, I did play with a buddy of mine who knocked himself out with his own tee shot. Here is that story plus 30 more true hacker's tales.

We arrived at the third hole on the Oak course at Middle Island Golf Course. A picturesque, yet treacherous, par four with the tee box aligned thirty degrees left of the fairway. Joe recognized this and adjusted his stance as he performed his pre-shot routine. He waggled and wiggled and bragged about how he was going to "wow the crowds". He "wowed" them alright. He hit a worm burner three inches off the ground that traveled ten yards forward and two to the left where, after a short bounce, it smacked into the wooden six inch square ladies tee box marker. The ball then launched itself about 5 feet 8 inches into the air straight back into Joe's forehead.

Joe stumbled like a drunk sliding off a bar stool at closing time. He wobbled for five or ten seconds before falling to his knees holding his head. Trying to suppress a chuckle, I rushed over to him. Seeing no blood, my attempt at acting concerned was no match for the primal instinct of uncontrollable laughter. With surprising agility, Joe dropped to his stomach, rolled onto his back and kicked me in the knee. Thus, I joined Joe on the ground with both of us rolling and moaning.

I recovered quicker than he did and forgave him for assaulting me. I helped him to his feet and together, we walked around the tee box a few times. He declined to re-tee and wisely chose to sit out that hole while he slowly regained a sense of awareness.

Being able to stand, partially see, and feebly swing the club, Joe was ready for battle on the fourth tee. However, despite it being a long Par 5, Joe opted to use a lofted iron and an extra long tee. He also made sure he placed his tee in line with the center of the forward markers!

"Nobody remembers the good golf shots; they remember the truly outstanding and the absurdly bizarre!"

3-Iron to the Skull

Working for a large corporation, playing golf is often essential for job security and advancement. Not to imply that this pervasive throughout Corporate America, but in some industries it is definitely prudent to know your way around a golf course. Al, my former boss, was fanatical about the game and could not comprehend how anyone could not be. Every Thursday and I mean every Thursday, be it raining, snowing or hot enough to boil the sweat off your brow, he would invite three of his subordinates to play golf with him. Invite being a very polite word.

Since there were eleven of us, our presence on the field of battle was requested at least once a month. Because Al and I were of comparable talent, I never complained and rather enjoyed these rounds. Joe, on the other hand, dreaded Thursdays. He fell ill many a Wednesday evenings and if given the choice of playing golf with Al or having his hair set afire, Joe would carry lighter fluid and a pack of matches in the pocket of his suit jacket.

Joe was the undisputed worst golfer in our entire department and he knew it. He also had a premonition that his job was in jeopardy due to his pitiful short game. On a morning that both he and I were "invited" to play with Al, Joe told me and Mark, the fourth member of our group, that if the opportunity arose, he was going to whack Al over the head with his 3-iron. In Joe's twisted mind, this would be a pre-emptive strike to buy him time to find another job in a new country.

Because Mark and I drove to the course together making the thirty minute trip in twenty-two minutes and eight seconds, Joe was forced to share a cart with his nemesis. Joe hated us for that. We, naturally, laughed. Prior to each round, Al would always suggest a friendly wager. His "suggestions", like his "invitations", were always accepted. We played two man best ball, cart versus cart. The round was progressing as expected. Joe would dribble his tee shot and Al would display mild disappointment. Joe would shank his approach shot into the nearest hazard and Al would look disgusted. Joe would blow an easy putt ten feet past the hole and Al would unsuccessfully try to suppress his anger.

Al's game was never at its best when he played with Joe and today was no exception. Down by three with five to play, Al hit his tee shot into the woods. He stopped the cart on the edge of the tree line and went to retrieve his errant shot. Joe slowly rose from his seat, stepped out of the cart and grabbed a club from his bag. He turned toward me and Mark, raised the club over his head, smiled and laughed an evil little laugh. He turned back toward the woods and followed Al.

Al is a quick golfer. If your ball is lost, he'll give you three minutes, never more, to find it. With this being the case, Mark and I started to get concerned when four, and then five minutes passed with no sign of Joe or Al. Now, you may be wondering why Mark and I were still in our cart. Well, the "Al's Rules of Golf" prohibit a player from assisting his opponent in locating a lost ball. Being Al's opponents for the round, we sat and waited.

We were tempted to break the rule when, at the seven minute mark, Joe emerged from the woods. He walked out alone and…he was still smiling. Mark and I looked at each other in disbelief. Was there something red dripping from the head of Joe's 3-iron? How would we explain that the boss went missing playing golf? What did Joe do with his body and how were we going to protect our friend?

What seemed like an eternity, but was probably no more than 45 seconds, Al stormed out of the woods, grabbed a ball from his cart, dropped it and, aiming for the fairway, hit it back into the woods.

Joe's premonition, unfortunately, proved accurate and he was let go two months later. The reason for his dismissal was cited as "poor performance," but Mark and I know that the typist accidentally omitted the word "putting" from the middle of that sentence.

"Don't ever underestimate the power of golf."

The Albatross Wears a Toupee

Golf is a game of contrasts. During the same round, you can skull a shot into your partner's foot and, on the very next hole, smack a 270 yard drive dead center of the fairway. Two consecutive shots can be so drastically different that you can only shake your head in disbelief while trying to decide which one is more reflective of your true skill. Now add the element of multiple golfers in a foursome and the variety of shots increases exponentially. I've personally witnessed golfers knocking themselves silly after the ball they hit ricocheted off of a tree. I have also played with fellow hackers who hit miraculous recovery shots from behind the same tree that returned their last shot into their forehead.

But just how different can two shots be for one foursome during the same hole? The answer to that question is what makes golf such an entertaining pastime. An even more spectacular aspect of the game is that the players mentioned in the next paragraph could easily be interchanged with the improbable outcome being just as possible.

To illustrate the amazing diversity of shots that make up this truly spectacular game, conjure up the image of a tee box of a Par Five on a typical golf course. The white tee markers are at the very forward edge of the tee box. A foursome at these tees is going through their pre-game routine, no doubt haggling over who gets how many strokes and the nature of the wager for the round. My group is at the tips of the tee box, about 30 yards behind the aforementioned group. From where we stood, we could see the ceremonial tee being tossed in the air, thus establishing who would hit first. We could see three of the golfers pointing and jeering at the fourth guy who appears nervous having to hit the first ball of the round. We see three golfers moving to the side allowing the chosen first man to tee up his ball.

Waiting our turn, and curiously watching the group ahead of us, secretly hoping that at least one duffs their shot into the rough, my foursome decides to warm up a bit. Neil, a 300 pounder who consistently hits 300 yard drives out of bounds, is practicing his swing with a seven-iron. Bob, John and I knew how far Neil could drive a ball, but we were unaware as to how far he could smack a divot. How fortunate for us that on this particular day, we would learn just how far. Taking a full swing at the ground, pretending that he was trying to crack an imaginary ball in half, Neil lifted a divot about the size of a full grown beaver tail and propelled it towards the white tees and one very unsuspecting golfer.

Quick question…do you yell fore for an incoming divot? We were not sure either, so we watched in stunned silence while the divot flew gracefully in the air, flipping like a well tossed pancake until it landed perfectly, dirt side down, on the head of the golfer still going through his pre-shot routine. It took several minutes, but the last of the laughs finally subsided and the group in front of us began their round without further interruption. The fact that they were amused rather than annoyed typifies the calm demeanor often displayed on the first tee but lost by the third green.

When it was our turn to take swings at a ball, Bobby, the unflappable member of our group, hit a monster drive rendering this par 5 definitely reachable in two. Still laughing about Neil's toupee shot, the rest of us hit unspectacular shots injuring several worms and other ground dwelling creatures.

The fairway sloped down and to the right. There was a water hazard down the left side of the fairway, starting about 100 yards from the first cut of the green and extending around the side and behind the putting surface. There were traps to the right of the green and another one short and slightly left of the green's centerline. John, Neil and I hit a few shots apiece before reaching the spot where Bob's drive landed. We were well rewarded by the splendid view we had of the first hole's flag.

If the view we had could be described as nice, Bob's second shot was the image of absolute beauty. It landed in the throat of the approach to the green and rolled onto the dance floor and towards the pin. We all expected it to fall short and to the right. But it rode a slight ridge on the green and picked up speed while homing in on the flagstick.

When the ball vanished from sight, Johnny jumped out of the cart screaming, "It's in the hole, it's in the hole!" Neil gunned our cart and we raced to the green. Bob just shrugged his shoulders, wiped the dirt from the face of his club with a towel, and placed the club in his bag. He then leisurely lowered himself into his cart while waiting for Johnny, who continued to dance around like a banshee on amphetamines, to return to his seat.

Although the odds of making a double eagle, or an albatross as it is sometimes referred to, is estimated to be roughly a million to one, and actually much more difficult than a hole-in-one because it requires two fantastic shots, it has been done before. And although it is quite rare, it will happen again – several times on the pro tour each year. Despite the fact that it is not unprecedented, Bob is, as he should be, extremely proud of his accomplishment. But it is difficult not to feel a tad bit sad for Bob. For his moment to shine was overshadowed by Neil's toupee shot – a shot that may truly forever be considered one of a kind.

"With a seven-iron and some luck, the impossible is achievable."

The "Almost" Perfect Shot

The "almost perfect shot", we've all had several. You would give up the game if you did not have at least one every round or two. Usually it comes near the end of the round, which is a clear indication that the golf gods want you to return real soon for more punishment!

Remember your first birdie? Was it a good tee shot on a par 3? Or perhaps a series of well struck balls on a longer hole? Or maybe, it was like mine?

It happened on a 150 yard par three at the old Hauppauge Country Club on Long Island. There were trees to the right and a huge bunker in front. Long and left was a safe bet. So, naturally, I hit it short and right. It slammed into a green-side oak tree having a trunk as wide as a 55 gallon oil drum. Had the tree fallen, I would have been less surprised than I was with what the ball did after hitting the tree. It ricocheted off of several large branches and countless smaller ones, trying desperately to extricate itself from the grasp of this monstrous tree. It shot upward and sideways and finally hurled itself out of the tree and towards the green and the flagstick; it bounced liked a misshapen rubber egg and rolled to within 18 inches of the cup. I looked over that putt for a week and a half. I studied the grain, using a magnifying glass to look for any small dent or protuberance, damning all who preceded me for leaving spike marks. Finally satisfied with my read and having only moments of daylight left, I closed my eyes, jerked the club back and forth and nearly lipped the putt.

My playing partner swiped the ball. When I asked him for it, he mumbled something about giving up the ball being customary for one's first birdie. I was so elated with my accomplishment, that I did not question this theft of valuable property. A few days later, he presented me with a wooden plaque displaying the scorecard highlighting the "2", an old photo of myself looking quite perplexed and the ball, which was inset into a small cavity. It is truly a priceless, yet hideous, work of art that I treasure to this day.

How about your first hole-in-one? Well, if you are good enough or lucky enough to have admitted to having one, you're not a true hacker. Please give this book to someone more deserving! But if you are a hacker, I bet you've had some near aces. Perhaps one using another element of nature other than a tree. One that requires more creativity and a comical stroke of luck.

The 11th hole at Pocono Manor, the West Course, is short, real short. The card reads 90, it plays about 60. The reason being is that there is a 120 foot drop about ten feet forward of the tee box. Thick brush covers the steep slope until you reach the cart path. Between the cart path and the green is a stream. Trees block your view of the green except at the extreme right-hand corner of the tee box. But you want to stay left because the right is where the stream is at its widest and balls landing there plummet off into the swift moving water.

I teed off from the left. The rest of the foursome watched from the right. I quickly discovered that a half sand wedge with an open face would not provide enough distance to clear the stream. I knew I was all wet. But then, in unison, I heard three voices very close to me yell, "it's in the hole, it's in the hole!"

"Yeah, right," was my muted reaction.

"Wait," said Perry, "it didn't drop, it hit the pin. I think the pin stopped it from rolling in!"

We drove the carts down the steep path, my anxiety rising with each second that passed. I jumped from the cart and raced to the green. The ball was not in the hole. It was not leaning against the flag stick, but it was less than one ball width away! Not having the privilege of witnessing the flight path of the ball, I have no other option than to believe Perry who said it hit a flat stone in the center of the stream, bounced twenty feet into the air and onto the perfect spot of the green from which it rolled towards the pin. Just one more revolution! That's all it needed, how could I be so unlucky!

The fun is in the pursuit!

Arizona Fiasco

When my two brothers, both living in Arizona, picked me up at the airport, they were surprised to see me take golf clubs off of the luggage carousel. "Are those yours?" Dom the doctor asked. "No", I replied. "I have entered into a life of crime and this is my first caper." Steve, the hydrologist, not to be outdone by his older brother, asked "what are you going to do with them?"
"I was thinking fishing. They're not real good for catching them, but you can knock them senseless if you can get close enough".

"Although I'd like to see that, I doubt it would work given the density of the water," said Dom. "Not to mention the alteration of the swing path as the club strikes the surface", Steve chimed in.
"Or the actual location of the fish that is distorted due to the refractive properties of water," Dom continued.

After finally kicking that dead horse, Steve did ask "you really plan on playing golf this week?"

"Not just me. We are going to have a brother's outing!" I conjured up images of a leisurely round chatting and laughing with my brothers. I saw myself hitting spectacular drives and instructing them on how to do the same. Their visions were probably somewhat different, but they agreed to play if they could choose the course.

With all of the beautiful and challenging golf courses in Arizona, they insisted on playing a short nine-hole course because it was touted as being beginner friendly. Not having any clubs of their own, Doc and the water boy were forced to rent. The bags they were given held only six clubs: a driver, a putter, a wedge and three irons. The bag was black and very small with huge white glow in the dark lettering emblazoned down the entire front that read: R E N T A L.

Dr. Dom said that he should just tape a neon sign to his forehead that blinked the word "Loser". In retrospect, he did not have to do that.

Dom wore slip-on boat shoes and Steve wore red high top converse sneakers. Both wore tee shirts and neither wore socks. I added dress code to the list of things this course lacked. Insisting on using rock, paper, scissors instead of the traditional tee toss, our first argument ended when we saw "him" coming. A fourth was being added to our merry trio of misfits.

His bag was immense. The cart pulling his bag was bigger. It had three sets of wheels and heavy duty shock absorbers. Gadgets hung from every strap like ornaments on a Christmas tree. And "he" had the look of a real golfer. His hat, shoes, colored coordinated slacks and collared shirt all matched his glove! Intimidation and fear hit my brothers with the force of a 100 mile per hour wind gust. They pleaded with me, "Let him go ahead of us".

The offer was made. "Thank you," he replied, "but no, please go ahead - I need to stretch for a moment." He went on to say that his name was Jim and he was in Arizona visiting his parents. He did not know anyone local who played golf and he welcomed the company. He enjoyed friendly competition because he really wanted to become a great golfer.

I was confused; he had to know he would be playing with some hackers. Surely he could read the writing on the "bag"! I hoped that after he witnessed our, bound to be, comical tee shots, he would excuse himself, blaming a reoccurring gastrointestinal flare-up, and wait until we were out of sight before joining another group.

Dr. Dom started us off by hitting a worm burner 10 feet short of the red tees, which were located a mere 20 yards away. Steve got off, what he considered to be, a decent drive - nearly doubling the distance achieved by Dom. Feeling satisfied with his monstrous 35 yard smackaroo, he yielded the box to me.

Aiming to salvage some dignity for my family, I took a massive swing. Unfortunately, I got under it and it popped high into the air landing midway between the balls struck by my brothers. If Jim could muster up an eighty yard drive, he could double the output of the foursome!

He looked awkward addressing the ball. More accurately, it looked as if he was trying to tango with his driver. He was all wiggle and waggle and lacking dazzle. And the ball was teed up a little high. But who am I to comment. He took a mighty stab at the ball, thrusting his left leg out two feet from where it started. The ball sailed high into the air where it met up with the gust of wind that traumatized my brothers just minutes before. We watched the ball drift out of bounds, over the fence dividing the course from the rest of the civilized world. Away it sailed along with Jim's dreams of joining the pro tour.

The ball landed in the middle of the road and, due to the grade of the surface or divine intervention, took a horrific bounce away from us and the golf course. We lost sight of it, but we estimate that when it finally came to a stop, it had to be a good hundred yards behind us! Since he did not improve much throughout the round, I would like to think that we brought this poor unsuspecting soul down to our level. And I also have to believe that he may have been able to muster a recovery if it were not for what awaited him on the next eight holes – a menagerie of small creatures and follies you'll read about in "Ducks, Kittens and the Picture Perfect Shot".

Unforgettable rounds rarely involve bragging about your final score.

Blind Date

After three years of marriage and a job change, I found myself working for a company that incorporated golf in all of their management conferences. Intent on not being the worst golfer at these outings, I began practicing, playing and developing a passion for the game. However, that first year was difficult, my progression was slow and, although I accomplished my goal of not being the worst golfer in the company, I was still considered the top of the sludge in the bottom of the barrel.

My wife must have mentioned my new found love to her mother, for while visiting her in Florida my mother-in-law surprised me with an arranged golf date with a friend of hers – a nice Canadian gentleman she befriended at a bingo tournament. She also procured for me an ancient set of clubs borrowed from a neighbor. On the morning of the arranged date, I paced the house anxious to get to the course. Sensing this, my mother-in-law assured me that my playing partner would arrive shortly and we would arrive at the course before our scheduled tee time. Assuming that this friend of hers would be as ancient as the clubs I would playing with, I was content just knowing I would be hacking away for a few hours.

The ancient Canadian, who claimed to be 76, looked twenty years younger and was extremely fit. He had an air of self-confidence similar to what I've seen displayed by the single-digit handicappers in my company. He introduced himself to me and told me how excited he was to be playing with me. All of his peers insisted on playing the par three executive courses and he longed for a round with a true player who could unleash the power in a driver. I was not quite sure if I figured into this dream of his, but retrospectively – this was the first sign of a brewing disaster. While I contemplated his comments, he continued to ramble on about the course in such detail that it was evident he was not new to the game and he assumed that neither was I.

Not having time to hit the range, he would see my first swing on the course. He flipped a tee that landed with the tip pointing at me. His excitement was only slightly dampened when I declined to play skins. I thought to myself that I would reconsider after a few holes if our skills were comparable. Being a little nervous, as usual, on the first tee, I was relieved when my tee shot went about 100 yards straight down the middle. Being that the first hole was a par five, most accomplished golfers would not be happy with that shot. Being a newlywed hacker, I was quite satisfied. However, this satisfaction immediately turned to fear when my playing partner suggested I re-tee. Although confused and bewildered, I still managed to say with pride that I would play it where it lied.

As he warmed up a bit, I noticed that his poise and swing mechanics were impressive. When he proceeded to crush a drive that would take me another three shots to reach, I started wondering who exactly this family friend was. A quick summation of my round would go something like this: my first tee shot was one of my best drives of the day, my approach shots were uglier than a three-headed rat that looked quite attractive when compared to my performance on the green. After only two holes, his smile was gone, the spring in his step now resembled the shuffling of a man headed for the gas chamber and he seemingly lost the ability to speak.

After nine, he scowled at me and then growled, "Want to continue". I thought his head would explode when I said yes. Actually, I was thinking that this day could redeem some value if his head did indeed explode. But alas, it did not and my affirmative response to play the back nine that day still ranks as one of the worst decisions I've ever made. He returned to his pretension of being a monk and my level of play sunk even lower. Unbelievable does not come close to describing some of my shots. Every squirrel and rabbit within a mile ran for cover and even the birds seemed to disappear from the skies. It was truly was one of the most miserable rounds of golf I have ever played and this, I remind you, is from someone who shot 146 in a member-guest tournament. My photo appears in the pro shop at that particular club with a caption that I believe reads, "banned for life".

When we arrived back at my mother-in-law's house, he popped the trunk while the car was still rolling and it never did come to a complete stop as I jogged after him to retrieve my golf bag. When asked how the round went, I had to admit that he was an excellent golfer. I decided to omit the fact that he was an arrogant snob who was probably, at this moment, mad at himself for not putting the car in reverse while I was lifting my bag from the trunk. I'm sure he would have pleaded that it was a necessary act to prevent others from being tortured by the level of my play. Smiling, as if she should receive the Mother Teresa award for humanity, it was then that my mother-in-law decided to inform me that this particular friend was a former golf pro and I don't mean at a local club – I mean a card carrying retired PGA pro. She intentionally kept that fact from me because her friend was really looking forward to playing with someone with my skill and she did not want me to be nervous.

Looking directly at her with my eyebrows arched upwards, I asked, "And what, pray tell, did you tell him of my alleged skill level?" "Well," she excitedly responded, "he asked if I knew your handicap. I told him, 'I'm not sure, but he's wonderful!' He then asked me if you shot in the 90's or 80's. I didn't know what to say, so I think I said, 'no, he's much better than that'. Was that right?"

"Absolutely," I said. "Perfect answer, if we stopped at nine. But, that explains a lot." After a few drinks, I told her about the round and she promised to never set me up again. Wise woman!

**If you think you're bad, have a seat,
relax and grab a beer.
There's always someone worse!**

Buddy, can you Spare a Club?

Fern, a newlywed, was with her husband Perry visiting his parents in the Mecca of golf – Myrtle Beach. Not wanting to be separated from her husband for five hours on a beautiful Saturday, Fern joined Perry on the course. Not yet having her own set of clubs, she borrowed her mother-in-law's. Her mother-in-law was an excellent golfer for her age and a very fastidious woman. When she handed Fern the bag she said, "be very careful with these my dear, they are, with the exception of my son, my prized possession." Fern's response was a classic – "then, I shall treat them like I do your son."

Up to this point in her life, Fern was a range golfer. She accompanied Perry numerous times using his clubs to whack the ball in the general direction away from where she was standing. Under Perry's tutelage, she actually struck the ball quite well. However, she was a course virgin – never having set foot on an actual tee box. Perry likes to say that she was as familiar with a golf course as a polar bear is to a cactus farm. This became most evident greenside on the 14th hole.

Being about twenty feet from the fringe of the green, Perry told Fern to execute a little bump and run. With her reply, "Bump what and run where?" Perry explained, "use your 7-iron and bring the club back only half-way, but make sure you follow through, you don't want to ground the club, yet you also don't want to…"

Looking in her bag while Perry rambled on, Fern said "I don't have a 7-iron".

"Really," responded Perry. "That's odd, so use your 8-iron – it has slightly more loft than the seven, so you must make contact…"

"Nope, no 8-iron either".

"You have to have an eight! Every set, especially my mother's has an eight and a seven!"

"I think I may have left the eight by the green on the last hole. But I swear I never had a seven!"

Perry took off in the cart back towards the last hole. There was no way he could return his mother's clubs minus the eight-iron. He would have to replace the whole set for her and she would still blame every poor shot until the day she died on her new clubs. When Perry reached the 13th green, an old hacker was placing the flag back in the hole. He was holding a bunch of clubs. He saw Perry and smiled.

"Looking for these?" he said while offering Perry two clubs.

"Ah yes, my wife left them behind, thanks so much – the eight and the seven!"

Perry was not surprised. He just knew his Mother had a complete set. Relieved and grinning, he began to navigate the cart around the old gent and made it about ten feet when he heard,

"Wait, do you want the rest?"

Now, Perry was surprised. But that feeling quickly passed and was replaced by shock when he was handed a nine-iron, a pitching wedge and sand wedge.

The aged hacker explained, "I started finding them on every third hole, but when I found two on this last one – I figured she must be running low! I'm assuming she would have realized it when she was left with only a driver and a putter."

"Clubs seek freedom, let them fly!"

Ducks, Kittens and the Picture Perfect Shot

This is a follow-up to the "Arizona Fiasco" story which took place entirely on the first tee box of a nine hole course. As bizarre as that first hole may seem, the round never did approach normalcy as it progressed unchecked by reality for another three hours.

Since the course was packed with slugs and snails carrying golf bags, I mentally prepared myself to endure periods of anxious boredom between shots. But bored, I was not. While waiting on the second tee, my brother, Dr. Dom, looked skyward and spotted some duck. A fierce debate ensued with us arguing as to the proper word to describe a bunch of these feathered poop bombers. However, the duck did not care if we called them a flock, a gaggle or a swarm, when they landed about fifteen yards from where we stood. Although they were, to the casual observer, minding their own business, Dom felt compelled to chase them while imitating their waddle and quack. A few seconds of this behavior would have been humorous, but he continued for the entire time we had to wait before we could tee off, which was a very excruciating four or five minutes!

On the third tee box, the good doctor spied a small cat napping under a bench. He decided to pick up the little furry creature by the nape of its neck to demonstrate how he could temporarily evoke paralysis. With its four limbs flailing about, doc squeezed the cat's neck in such a way that it immediately went limp. When he relaxed his grip on the cat's neck, the flailing commenced. Squeeze... limp... relax... flail... squeeze... limp... relax... flail... Over and over he did this. Thankfully, we had to continue playing and his new found friend was allowed to run free. Amazingly, the cat looked up at the doctor and seemingly unfazed by what had happened, sauntered back to the bench to resume its nap.

Due to the absence of any wildlife, nothing else out of the ordinary occurred until the seventh hole. Despite the fact that we were walking, my dear brother decided that he was not getting sufficient exercise playing golf, so he thought it a good idea to do some jumping jacks, pushups and sit-ups. He chose the middle of the seventh green to do this. Since the course was slightly more congested than the Los Angeles freeway on a rainy Tuesday morning following a holiday weekend, the number of witnesses to his antics exceeded the population of several small African nations. Although we could make out some of the comments, we opted not to respond or offer an explanation.

On the last tee, Doc hit a nice drive. The first nice drive of the round and possibly one of his best ever. It really was a pretty shot - sailing perfectly down the middle of the fairway, bouncing several times and rolling gently to the center of the landing area. Without comment, the doc dropped his driver and triumphantly thrust both his arms straight up into the air and pumped his fists. Understandable? Perhaps a little over the top, but given the circumstances - somewhat justifiable. But what he did next was...almost inconceivable.

Again, without comment, he ran down the middle of the fairway leaving his club, bag and stunned playing partners behind. He did not stop at his ball, or the green - but continued to run off the course into the parking lot. We could not see what he was doing, but we did see him return to the course holding something in his right hand. He stopped at where his ball landed. He bent down over his ball and raised the object he was holding up to his face. With my brother Steve carrying two bags, we made our way to where Dom was now dancing. When I saw the camera in his hand and the grin on his face, I knew that was a picture worth having!

Much to my amazement, as well as his own, Dom shot par for the hole and with that he turned to Steve and I and with genuine sincerity said, "you want to play again?" Not knowing, or wanting to know, what we could expect during a second nine, we graciously declined.

Look beyond the obvious to find the miraculous!

El Guappo

Craig, a.k.a. El Guappo, carried his golf bag like you and I carry a bowling bag. He uses his pitching wedge inside 150 yards and can hit his long irons over 250 yards. His drives go further, much, much further, but seldom straight. The severity of his slice is legendary. Rumor has it that he sliced a drive so bad that the flight path of the ball resembled that of a tossed boomerang. The ball traveled well over 300 yards ending only about 20 yards from the spot from where Craig stood.

El Guappo and I were playing a quick nine. He had his slice under control, which he did by aiming his drive forty-five degrees left of the center of the fairway. After only seventy-five minutes, we stood on the eight tee. The eighth hole on this course has trees extending from the tee box for about 100 yards down the right-hand side of the fairway. Beyond the trees, it is wide open with the seventh fairway adjacent to ours. From the 8th tee, the tee box for the 7th hole is about 320 yards South and 100 yards West. Using Pythagoreans' theorem that we learned in High School algebra, we can estimate that the distance from Craig to the 7th tee box was about 335 yards away.

A water hazard lined the left-hand side of the fairway, so El Guappo naturally aimed for the center of the pond. The ball started left, but quickly began drifting right, clear of the water, clear across the fairway and clear of the last tree in the right rough. We moved quickly forward in an attempt to follow the path of the ball. When we could see beyond the trees, we spotted the ball still traveling in a Southwesterly direction, we also saw a foursome on the 7th tee box. Craig's heat seeking missile shot was homing in on them. We screamed "fore", "duck" and "holy shit", but sound can only travel so far.

The ball landed, traveling at a terminal velocity just shy of the maximum speed achieved by the space shuttle at launch, one inch above the right eye of a Yeti. Now you can imagine that someone who carries his golf bag like a lunch pail is big. And El Guappo is big. However, the guy he felled also looked big and we were still over 300 yards away from where he was staggering. Approaching him in our cart we noticed that he looked incredibly large from 200 yards and absolutely huge at 100. His staggering ceased and he fell, taking several seconds for his head to reach the ground. Lying there, he resembled a toppled gnarly old oak tree.

His playing partners were stunned; they stood there speechless. They looked at us as if we just slain the dragon that had terrorized the kingdom for decades. But death was not in the cards that day and big foot slowly made it to his feet. We gave him a small bag of ice and a cold beer that we coincidentally had with us. The ice was a coincidence, the beer was a given. He chugged the beer, put the ice on his cheek and said "hazards of the game." He put the ice on the seat of his cart, grabbed a club and proceeded to tee off!

We skipped the rest of the 8th and the entire 9th hole just in case Sasquatch had a change of heart and decided to hunt us down.

**Hitting the ball is routine,
what you hit with the ball is entertainment.**

Follow the Bouncing Ball

"That's the worst shot I've ever seen!"

Fact: all of us have seen one, but can you recall it and can you really be convinced that it was truly the worst shot you have personally witnessed? What you need is something to compare it to. You need a standard from which all other ugly shots can be judged. If your standard is surpassed by one that is worse, the new shot becomes the standard. Sort of like king of the hill. If the original is more unique, comical, bizarre or horrific – it remains on the top.

Not sure where to start? Feel free to use this one as the current king…

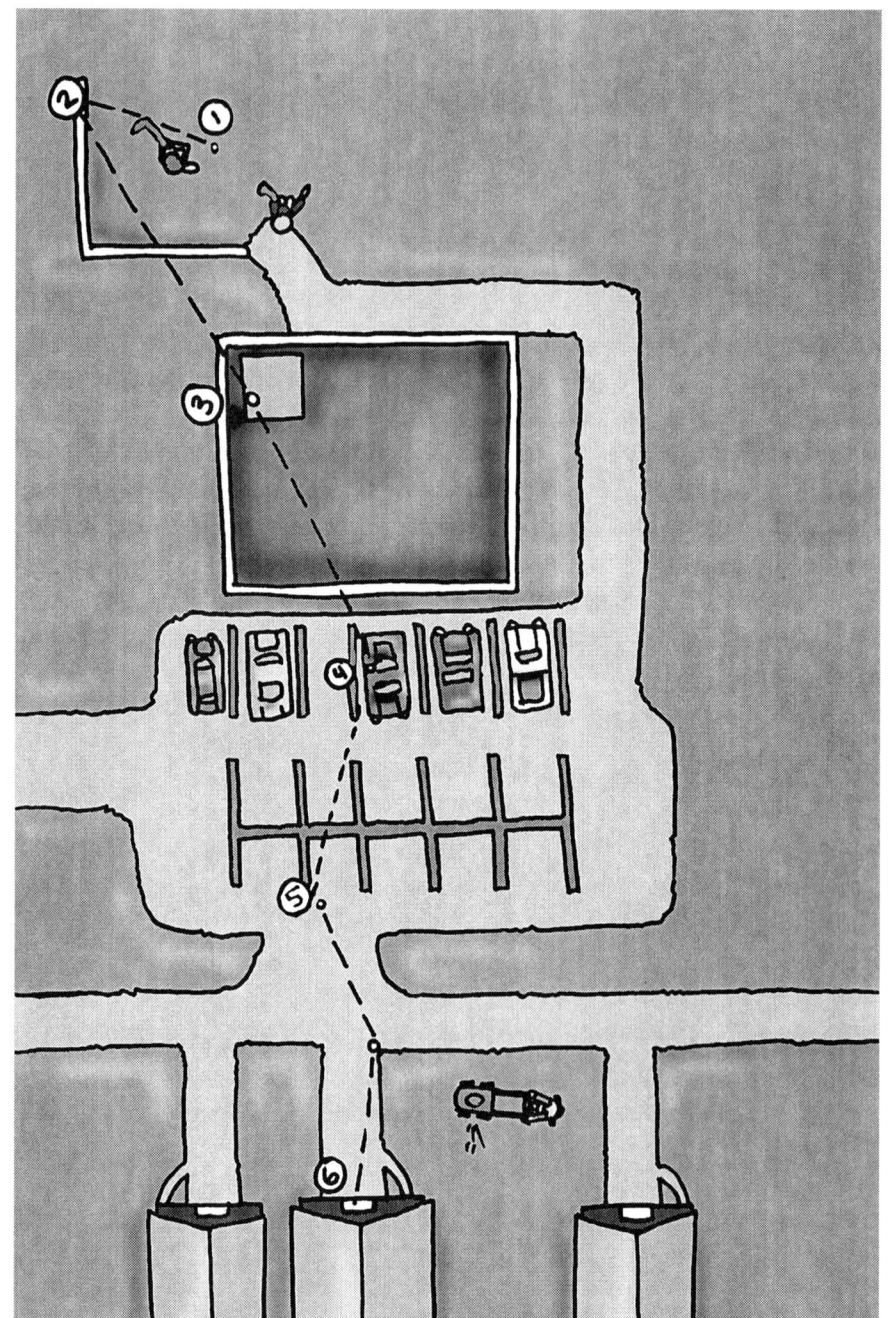

(1) Standing on the 1st tee, the entire golf course lies to the West and North. A chain-link fence separates the course and a road. Near the tee, the fence curves inward to help keep balls from bombarding passing cars. My tee shot was high and left.
(2) It hit the top of the fence, right under the curve and careened off to the North.
(3) It bounced on the flat roof of the clubhouse and then hit the air conditioning unit on such an angle that it was propelled eastward.
(4) It rolled off of the roof and into the parking lot where it miraculously missed ever car. Gary, my playing partner was following it's every move with commentary that even the great McCord would be proud of. I chased Gary to the parking lot to witness this extraordinary feat of vehicle avoidance.
(5) The ball continued to roll out of the parking lot, across a street and up the driveway of a home located on the opposite side of the road.
(6) We ceased our pursuit, hiding behind a van while spying a bemused home owner curiously watching the ball roll past him and his lawn mower. The ball's journey finally ended in the garage – no doubt looking for its brethren. The man with the mower looked around, scratching his head, no doubt asking himself where the heck that could have come from.

Seeing that no damage resulted from this errant shot, we returned to the 1st tee and the round recommenced with a fair degree of normalcy.

It's all about the journey!

Four Wedge Challenge

"Four wedges, are you kidding me? And why", asked Perry, "are your clubs in your garage?"

"The pros carry four and I was cleaning out the trunk of my car," was my dignified response.

I knew Perry would not leave it at that, so I prepared myself for some abuse.

"Well," he began, "you need a shovel to get out of a trap, your lob wedge only gets you in trouble and you hit your pitching and attack wedges the same exact distance – twenty yards short of your target."

"Not true, I am a master with my lob wedge. I can clear just about anything with this 65 degree magic club!"

What followed was "The Great Four Wedge Challenge". The concept was simple. We would each place a ball in front of an object and gracefully strike the ball to clear the obstacle. Three tries would be allowed for each object. The first one not to clear an obstacle by the third attempt would lose and pay for lunch.

Since we could not just walk out onto a course and start hacking away, we went to the biggest park within twenty miles to prove who was the "wedge wizard" and who was the "wedge weenie". The park we selected was perfect. There was a large boulder, numerous trees, a back-stop behind a baseball diamond, a small brick building, swings, hedges and light poles to illuminate the ball fields. We quickly put them in height order.

We would start with the four foot high hedge and then move onto the boulder that stood about six feet high. The swings with a top height of eight feet would be next and then the brick building at ten feet. These would be easy warm-ups which we could make more difficult if we placed the ball close to the base of each. The fifteen foot high handball wall and the back-stop, with its peak being about twenty feet in the air, would be the next two obstacles.

Out of the numerous trees to choose from, we selected two forty-foot ones that stood side by side far away from the rest of their fauna friends. Plus, there was a nice landing area for our errant shots. Our last obstacle would be the lights. They were easily 60 feet at the pinnacle.

After a few practice shots, we conquered the hedge, the boulder, the swing and the building using only one shot apiece per obstacle. Our confidence surged as we headed for the handball court. This was going to be a little tricky, not due to the height but because we needed to start from a grassy spot behind the fence that protected the court. We both missed on our first attempt, but succeeded on our second.

Perry cleared the backstop on his first shot, but I came up short. I blamed it on my lie. The taunting from Perry was merciless. My second shot hit the very top and rolled back down towards us. I thought I would cave-in to Perry's relentless attack. He had already crowned me the "wedge weenie" and made up some ridiculous lyrics to accompany my new title. But on my final attempt, I hit a beauty – kissed my club, turned to Perry and, with a smirk, said "shall we continue".

The trees that we spotted from a distance were not 40 feet high. They were at least fifty and they were gnarly mean looking elm. The top of the two trees connected to form a canopy that covered a quarter of an acre! "Perhaps we should skip the trees," I suggested. "Chicken wedge weenie," was Perry's reply. I should have seen that coming.

So we tried and failed, tried again and failed and then, miraculously I cleared them! I celebrated and smugly turned toward Perry ready for him to concede to my wedge striking prowess. But, he shrugged, rolled his eyes and hit a perfect third shot. "Just toying with you," he said.

And off to the lights we went. I suggested we hit from behind the lights and into centerfield. Since the baseball field was vacant and there would be plenty of room to land our shots. But Perry insisted we start in centerfield. He thought the grass was nicer and watching the ball sail over the lights into the vast beyond would make for a nice finishing shot.

For fear of being called chicken wedge weenie again, I did not want to confess that I feared striking and breaking a light.

In retrospect, I should have expressed my concern and faced the certain abuse I would receive from Perry. But I did not, so I felt a small pang of guilt when his first attempt came up ever so slightly short and, after a small explosive sound, shards of glass began to sprinkle to the ground.

Being the "wedge weenie" that he is, he ran! I followed quickly, being that he drove and walking home was not an option. Since I was not given the chance to attempt the last obstacle, Perry admitted defeat and I enjoyed one of the best lunches I've ever had – wienerwurst and potato wedges!

Having the right equipment will get you half way there. Knowing how to use them will get the ball in the hole.

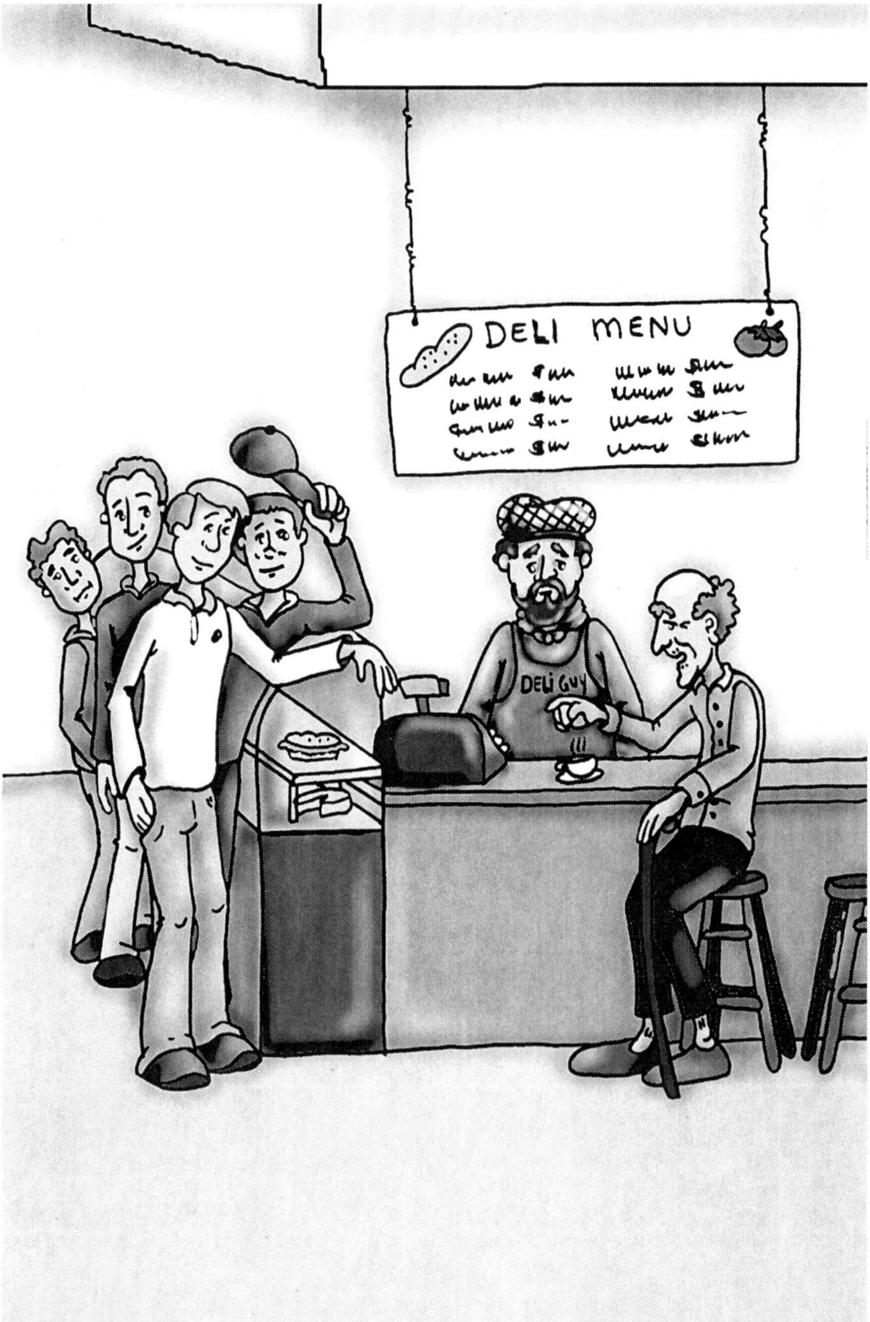
DELI MENU
DELI GUY

Go to Gull Haven

Prior to the welcome proliferation of golf courses on Long Island, spur of the moment golf and the weekend mixed as well as the Hell's Angels at a champagne and caviar cotillion.

But despite the odds of getting out on a sunny Sunday morning without a reservation being roughly the same of getting hit by lightning while rolling a yahtzee, a few beers convinced the four of us to meet at five the next morning. We rolled our eyes at the thought of others golfers actually beating us to the course!

We arrived at the West Sayville golf course and saw only a few cars! There was a clock by the club house with the small hand pointed at the five and the big hand at the twelve. Upon seeing that, Scotty exclaimed, "a five-hour round, I can handle that!"

Our optimism soared upon hearing that a four-hour round was the actual expectation, but it crash landed upon learning that the clock was the wait time. In our drunken stupor, we had forgotten about pre-paid tee times.

"Let's try Timber Point," said Steve. "They have three nine-hole courses and no pre-paid tee times, I think."

It was a splendid thought and we confidently drove the five miles to the course. The wait there was four and a half hours, but we did receive some useful, albeit sarcastic advice, to call in advance to reserve a tee time like everyone else who showed up to play that morning.

"Well. It's getting better", said Scotty.

"It's getting later", said Joe. "Let's call a few courses instead of traveling around like hobos."

Although I did not personally know any hobos, especially any who played golf, I also thought calling made sense. So we did…Middle Island, Swan Lake, and Rock Hill – all booked solid. The pro shop attendant at Spring Lake actually laughed at us when we said we wanted to play today. Dejected, we decided that breakfast would cheer us up.

We stopped at a deli that had stools lined up in front of the counter. We ordered some egg, ham and cheese sandwiches with coffee and started to commiserate. An old gent, probably no more than 90, and certainly no less, evidently overheard our conversation. With a voice that could never be mistaken for anything other than a 90 year-old hacker, he coughed and sputtered and slowly spoke, "Gooo toooo G u l l H a v e n n n n".

We looked at each other and then looked around and again heard… G oooo t ooo G u lllll H a v e n n…

When we identified the source of the sound, he lifted a long bony finger and pointed to the west wall of the deli. "Da o l d lelele loooony b i n, dats wh e r e ya'llll find er" and then he returned to his coffee.

Puzzled, we looked at the deli clerk. He enlightened us, because the old guy was evidently done talking. "There is in fact", he told us, "a public course on the grounds of the abandoned psychiatric hospital a few miles up the road. It used to be reserved for hospital staff. When the hospital closed, the course was opened to the public. Not many people are aware of that, so you have a shot of getting out this morning."

"What the hell," said Scotty, "let's go!".

Ten minutes later, we arrived at the course only to find two cars in the parking lot.

"Figures," said Joe, "it's closed".

"Let's go see," said Scotty.

Approaching the entrance gate, Joe threw his hands up in the air, "Wonderful, look at the sign – it says members only."

"No problem," says Scotty, "we'll join!"

Scotty was the optimist in the group, Joe the pessimist with me and Steve too hung over to argue. We followed Scotty's lead.

The ancient guy from the deli's older brother was in the pro shop. The pro shop was the same size as the trailer of an eighteen-wheeler. In fact, it was the trailer of an eighteen-wheeler. Directing his comments to Mr. Negative, the ancient one spoke first, "You members?"

"Well, no, but…"

"That will be eleven dollars then."

"So, we can play?"

"If you give me $11 dollars."

"To play?"

"You guys been drinking?"

"Well…, not this morning, but…"

"This is a nine-hole course. If you fork over $11, you can play twice. First nine from the white tees, second nine from the blue tees. Next to the putting green there is a spiral. You put your ball in the top of the spiral and when your ball reaches the bottom, it is your turn to tee off. You must let waiting members tee off before you and if any members are starting their second nine, you must let them play through."

We paid $11 each, slightly more than we would have paid to play miniature golf and headed for the spiral.

The spiral could safely accommodate 50 golf balls. There were none presently in the spiral. There were no golfers on the practice green, there were no golfers on the ninth green, there were no golfers anywhere! But, doing as we were told, we put our ball in the top of the empty spiral and watched it roll down to the bottom. We retrieved it from the bottom of the spiral and headed for the first tee.

We played a leisurely 18 holes in excellent time, spotting a few other golfers, but not actually coming into contact with any. From that day forward, we vowed to make Gull Haven our home course.

Unfortunately, word spread about the Gull. The full page ad in the local paper didn't help and that course joined the other with membership drives, paid tee times and advance reservations. But on that one beautiful Sunday morning, the course was ours and we, even Joe, enjoyed every moment!

**Have confidence and good
fortune will follow.**

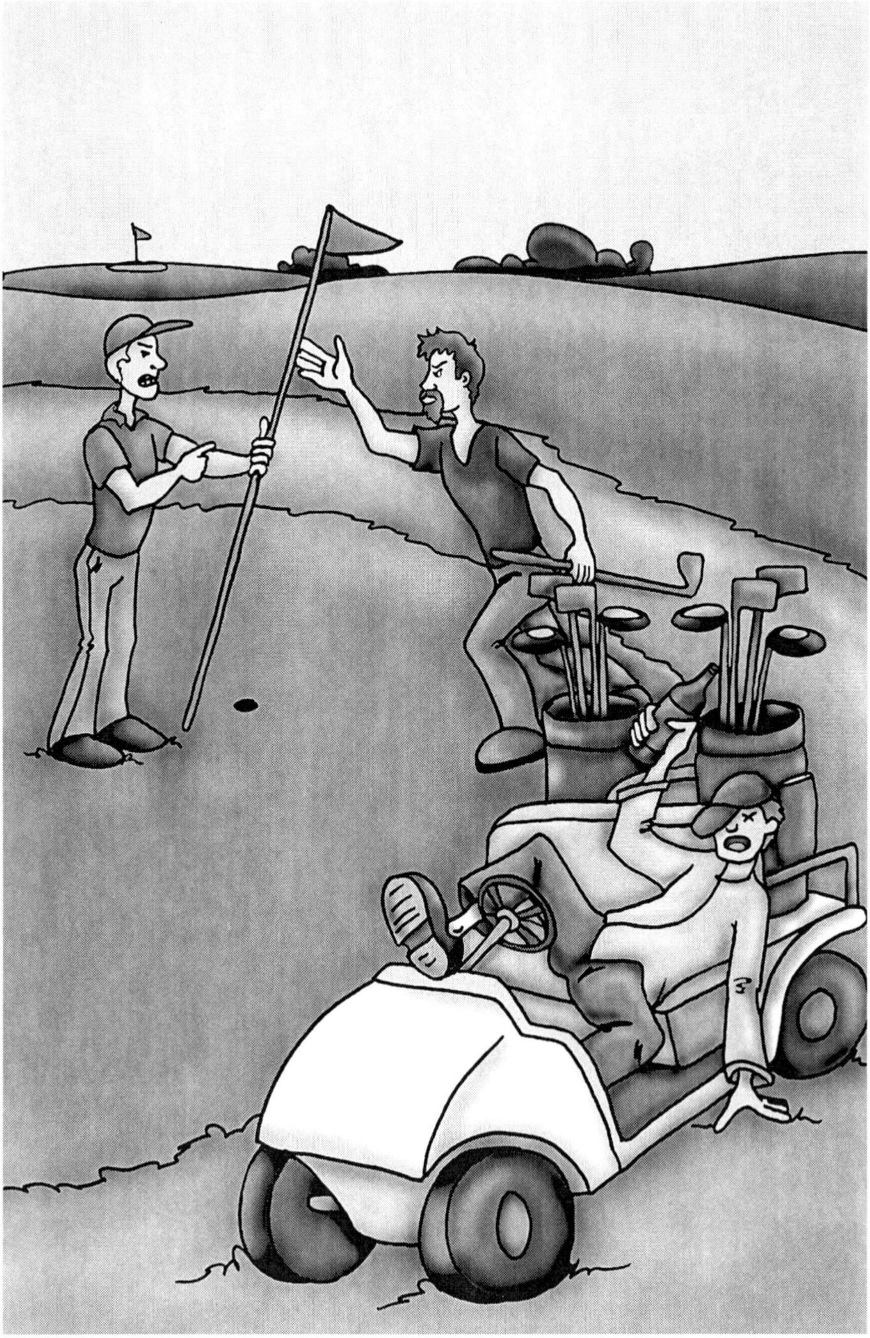

Have a shot

While vacationing in the Dominican, my friend Craig and I played golf in the late afternoon with a local caddy. His name was Jose. He was in his early thirties and slight in stature - weighing no more than 130 pounds. I happened to have a bottle of good tequila with me, Don Patrone Gold. I ceremoniously opened it on the first tee, pulled two plastic shot glasses from by golf bag and offered a shot to Craig. When Jose saw the bottle, he started salivating. The beer in the Dominican is excellent, but a good bottle of Tequila is hard to come by. I conferred with Craig and we agreed that should either of us get a par or better on a hole, Jose could indulge.

Well, Craig and I played some of our best golf ever. We had a string of pars that would impress the average hacker. And Jose had a shot for every one of them. After the first five or six, I told Jose that he was not obligated to drink and the option to do so was entirely his. Not once during the remainder of the round did he opt not to have a shot. By the time we reached the fourteenth hole, Jose was in great spirits. Between spates of laughter, he would point to something and dispense some incomprehensible advice.

Due to the heat, carts are obligatory. The golf bags remain on the cart and the caddies only carry the putters. Our putters were in the bags on the fifteenth hole and Jose was in our cart on the sixteenth. It was at this point that he pretty much ceased to be of any use to us. I walked the last few holes while Craig tried, unsuccessfully, to keep Jose upright.

The bottle was empty when Craig and I carried Jose to the Caddy shack at the end of our round. We gave him a handful of pesos. We figured if your caddy can help you out for most of the round and make you laugh for the rest, he deserves a nice tip.

Craig and I decided to play the same course the next morning. We restocked our bag with new balls and another bottle of tequila. We stopped at the caddy shack and asked for Jose. The caddy master shook his head and said, "No Jose, Jose no come to work today, he not feeling well".

Hmmm…I wonder why?

"We are what we drink."

He Stole my Putter!

Alan has played golf with a caddy. He has walked while a caddy carried his bag and he has walked while a caddy carried both his bag and another golfer's bag. But this was the first time Alan rode in a cart while also using a caddy. Alan hit the first drive of the day dead center of the fairway. His approach shot landed thirty yards short of the green and his chip shot left him with a fifteen-footer for par. Confident that he would take the first hole, and first skin, from me, he drove his cart up near the green. He stepped out of the cart and back to his bag to grab his putter. He panicked. His putter was missing. Thinking he left it on the practice green when he decided to bump and run a few eight-irons from the fringe, he curses and berates himself while walking back and forth from the green to his cart – hoping that it miraculously found its way into my bag. Around and around the cart he walks, each time checking his bag as he passes by.

On the green, he finds his caddy holding out a putter. "Thanks, I could use that, I seemed to have misplaced mine." He takes the putter from the caddy and exclaims "Wow, this is the same putter I lost!" Thinking he is joking around, the caddy smiles and points to a spot where Alan should aim his putt. Alan sinks the putt and pumps his arms upwards and slightly away from his body, thus extending the putter towards the caddy. When the caddy reached for the putter, it was hard to determine who had a more confused look on their face - the caddy with his hand grasping for the club or Alan who pulled it back towards himself clutching it like it was the last dollar he owned.

Alan reluctantly handed over the club and walked back to the cart looking around, I assume, to see if another putter would drop from the sky. He turned to say something to me just when I handed my putter to my caddy. He stammered, emitting some prehistoric guttural sound and then his eyes lit up. "Oh, I get it," he said, "They carry your putters for you!"

**Golf is a game that takes a lifetime to learn.
Lesson number one, trust your caddy.**

I never liked that club anyway!

Every golfer, at one time or another, has thrown something out of frustration. After a few bad shots, followed by a miserable putt, it is only natural to blame the ball. "It has an asymmetrical deformity!" Into the woods it goes.

I have witnessed a fellow hacker by the name of Jeff fling his entire golf bag into a water hazard. I have also witnessed a fellow hacker by the name of Jeff retrieve his bag from a water hazard.

Hats, gloves and towels also get flung. But it is the club that receives the most abuse. See a club in pieces in the woods or in a trash can on the course, suppress the urge to believe it was accidental. Sure, the golfer may not have wanted to break it when he bent it over his knee or wrapped it around a tree - but he probably should have expected that as a possible outcome.

Now, granted, there are pure accidents. I have seen my fair share of club heads decapitating and launching themselves from the shafts. This does happen, although not as often as it did with the old wooden head drivers, which when separated from the shaft, would often travel further than the ball it last struck. Unintentional club tossing also occurs. Take, for example, Dave. Dave knew his grips were worn but he never had time to have them re-gripped. He found time after his driver left terra firma and found itself in the canopy of a large elm tree. The club landed so high in the tree, that you could not see it. Despite some valiant and innovative attempts, Dave never did recover that driver, never! It is rumored that it provides support for a beautiful osprey nest.

But, by far, the greatest club toss in modern history may be attributed to Scotty. On the third hole at Gull Haven, Scotty sculled two consecutive shots with his three-iron. After the second shot traveled 23 feet on a ninety-degree angle into the rough, Scotty twirled like a ballerina with his 3-iron held out like a sword. On his third twirl, he let the club fly. It sailed over a fence that separated the course from a recently closed psychiatric facility and smashed through an unopened second floor window. If he tried, with all the remaining clubs in his bag, I bet he could not duplicate that throw! That is not, however, the end of the story.

Upon conclusion of our round, Scotty went to the Pro Shop and asked if anyone had found a 3-iron, leaving out the part that it was last seen trying to admit itself into a closed insane asylum. "Check those out," replied the attendant while pointing to a bunch of clubs huddled together in a corner. I am not proud to say that Scotty wasted no time selecting one and announcing that he had found "it". The fact that "it" was neither the correct brand nor a 3-iron is conveniently omitted from the "Hacker Record Book" where Scotty is listed under the entry of longest golf club toss.

Hit them, smash them, throw them and snap them, but can you really ever truly hate them?

It's a Gimme!

I always enjoyed playing golf with Scotty "no-show". Yes, the same Scotty who holds the club toss record. But since he rarely shows up at the course when promised, a round with Scotty "no show" is indeed rare. But if you ever have the pleasure to play with Scotty, I offer this advice – play cart golf with him as your partner.

Scotty has a strange short game. He can chip it close to the hole like nobody I've ever seen! He can also lag putt within a foot more frequently than most professionals on the tour. Being that this aspect of his game is so good, he is horrendous off the tee and is thus a solid double bogey golfer. Now, I did say Scotty can get it close to the hole and that is true, however that last foot or so is fodder for controversy. He'll usually scoop it away when he hears "that's good", so Scotty rarely gets to hear the ball clink off the bottom of the cup. The absence of that sound and his understanding of "that's good" is what separates "Mr. No Show" from the great horde of hackers.

During one memorable round, during which Scotty and I were cart partners in a match, he easily left a half a dozen long putts within a few inches of the cup. All six were "gimmes" and Scotty picked up without tapping in. I might also add that on all six of these holes our opponents questioned Scotty's score. "No show" would always look back toward the fairway, point to various trees and bunkers, and come up with a number that was accepted, although, with a certain degree of suspicion.

After a fairly difficult Par four, Scotty carded a 5 and we won the hole. Since every one of our shots was eerily similar on that hole, and I ended with a 6, I whispered to Scotty, "are you sure you got a 5?" After he said yes, I described each of his first four shots and ended with "and two putts makes six". He countered with, "no, I only had one putt".

"No," I said, "you had that unbelievable putt and the gimme". To which he replied, with all sincerity, "yeah, but the gimme doesn't count".

Perhaps I should have told him that his interpretation of a gimme had inherent flaws, but we were up by one with four to play and besides that, my mind started wandering…."so, in Scotty-Golf, you can get a hole-in-one without actually hitting the ball in the hole. Hmmm, how many hole in ones would I have? Let's see there was that one time at Pocono Manor when…."

I decided not to tell him until the next time we played and after I took a seat in the other cart!

**"Never let the number of strokes you take,
or don't take, dictate how well you played."**

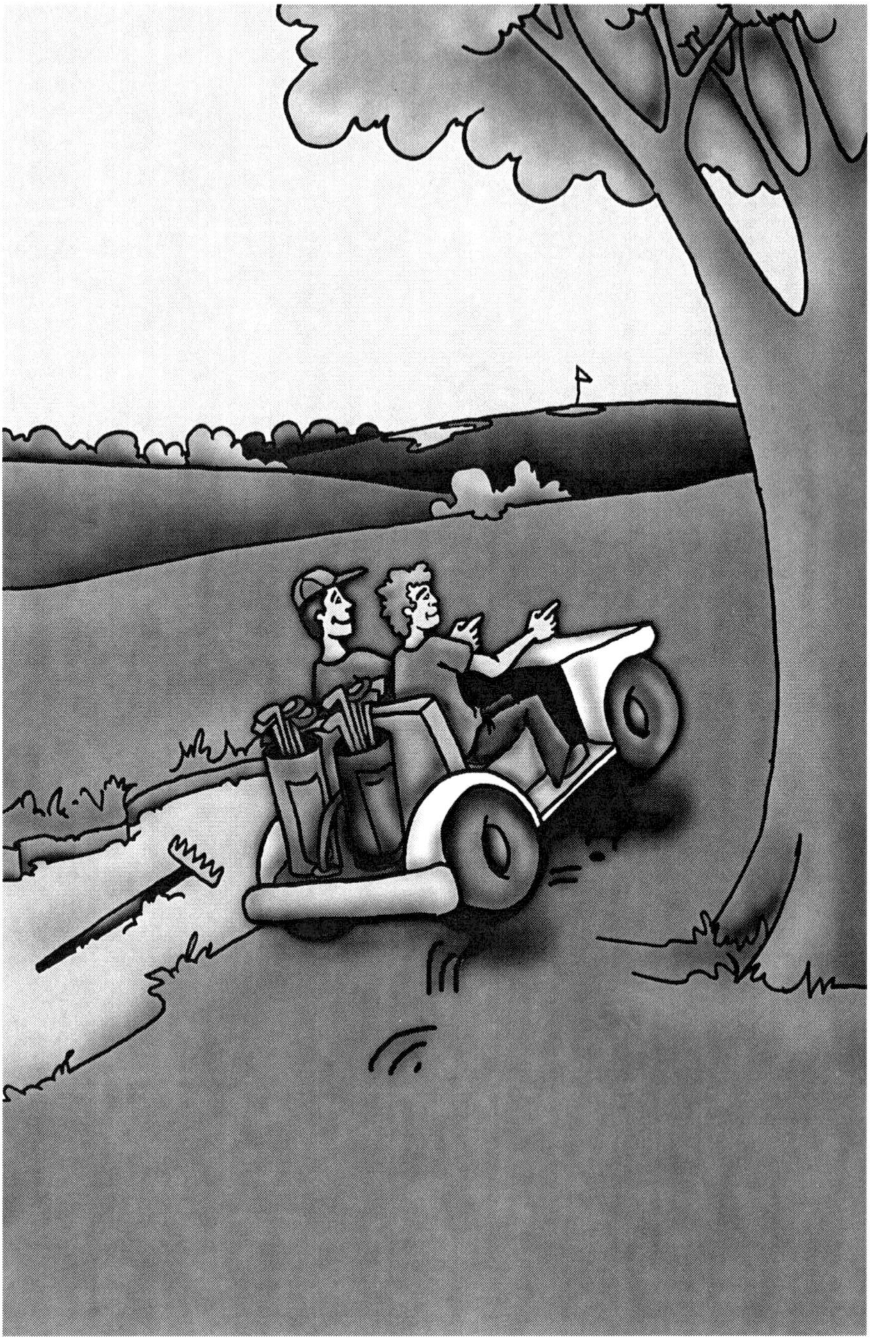

Keep your eyes on the road and your hands upon the wheel…

Don's tee shot was as long as any I have personally witnessed. And it was straight, perfectly straight. Problem was, the hole was a dog-leg left and his drive cleared what he thought to be an unreachable bunker situated on the right edge of the turn. So over the bunker and through the woods to Grandma's house Don went in search of his ball with Simon driving the cart.

Simon drove slowly down the tree-line. Don, like most hackers, envisioned his ball hitting a huge oak and being knocked back into play. After a quick survey of the fairway squashed that dream, both Simon and Don focused their attention to the right and in the woods as they approached the bunker. The cart climbed a slight incline with both occupants craning their necks looking out the right-hand side of the cart. Slowly upward the cart moved as Don and Simon continued scanning right. Up to the crest of the bunker they slowly rolled. Slowly upwards they went with eyes fixed to the right. Up, up, up the cart climbed and then…quickly downward it rolled into the center of the trap.

John and I were on the opposite side of the fairway witnessing this in slow motion. Not quite sure what to yell, we merely looked upon the scene in fascinated silence. Miraculously, the cart did not flip and luckily, there was no lip on the leading edge of the bunker. Driving the cart out of the bunker was easy, but armed with all the rakes we could gather, it still took us five full minutes to smooth it out!

A Search is never a waste of time because you'll find what you're looking for in the last place you look.

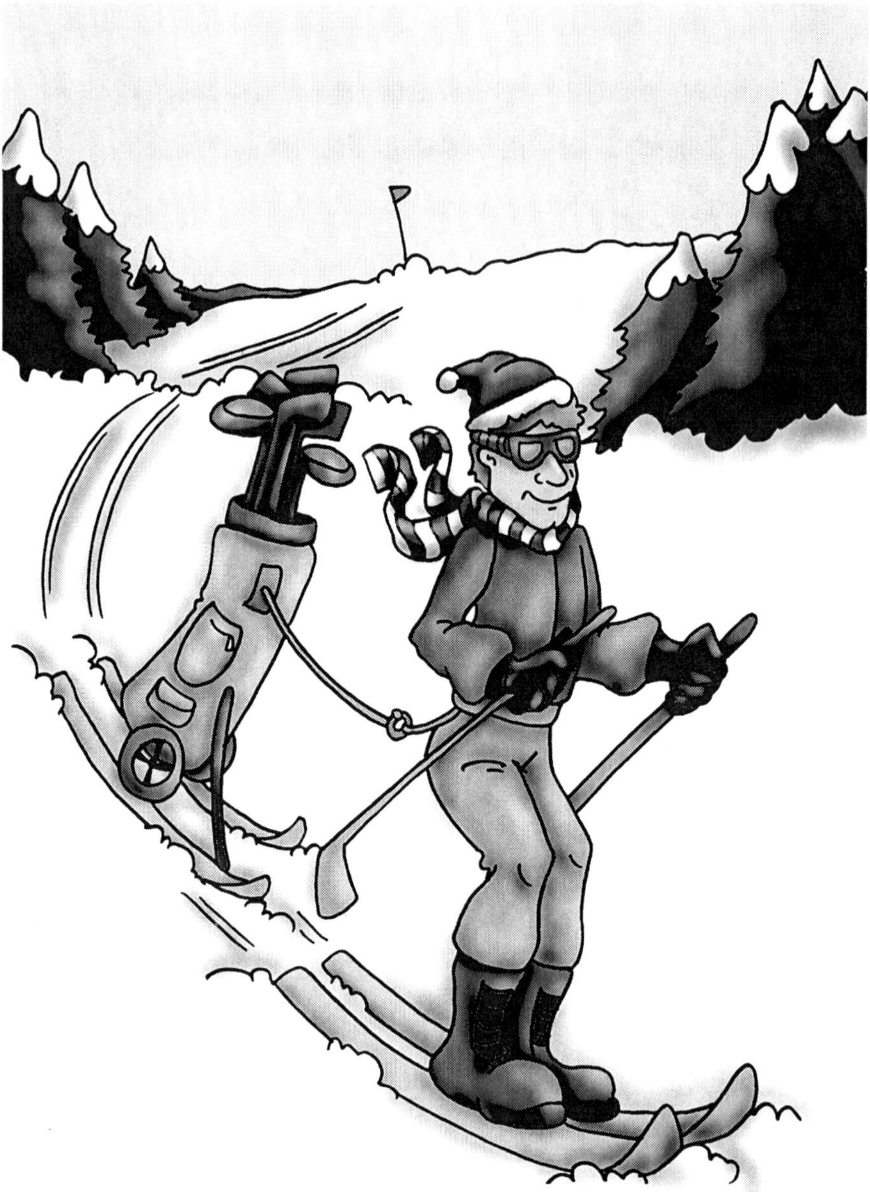

The Lady in Pink

Chris is a surfer. Chris is a fantastic surfer. He is also a damn good skier. On the golf course, Chris is...well, Chris is.., well he's a damn good skier. When he found himself two feet from the out of bounds marker, with trees and an elderly woman in a pink shirt gardening in the small yard behind her townhouse to his right, Chris should have stood perpendicular to the fairway and punched it out of the woods. But, by challenging the golf gods and attempting a miraculous shot down the tree line and towards the green, he most certainly assured himself that the shot would careen off the toe of his club, bounce off a few trees, and ultimately travel in the opposite direction of its intended path. Which, of course, it did.

Defying the laws of physics, the tree, not knowing any better, sent the ball back and to the left at a velocity speed roughly three times faster than what the club was capable of achieving. Not knowing exactly where the ball was headed, we all scrambled for cover behind the carts.

We heard the rustling of the leaves and tree branches and then a thud. We looked in front of us, but saw no ball. We looked left, but saw no ball. We looked behind us and then to the right where we saw a pink shape lying on the ground.

"Good Lord, he killed her!" screamed Don.
"This is not good," was all John could muster.

I joined them and we all rushed over to her side. The thought of not wanting to see my first fresh dead body was thankfully replaced with a sigh of relief. She was not dead, but rather kneeling close to the ground inspecting her new plants. We smiled and left her, alive and well, hoping that the shock of seeing three grown men with golf clubs surrounding her didn't give her a heart attack.

The 50:50:90 rule states that when faced with a decision having only two possible outcomes, each with an equal chance of occurring, you will choose wrong 90% of the time.

Larry's Trick Shot

In Arizona, many of the golf courses have tee boxes that are separated with undisturbed desert rendering most balls hit there unplayable. On one particular 367-yard par four, the area between the championship and men's tees is really ugly - cactus and scrub brush covering 70% of the expanse with the barren ground covered with crushed rock, discarded clubs and the remains of lost hackers. Fortunately, we were playing from the men's tees, so that area was of no concern to us. All we had to do was carry about 120 yards of slightly less intimidating terrain to reach the plush fairway.

Larry, the best golfer in the foursome, has a habit of quickly bringing his club back after completing his swing. The club normally would follow the same path as his actual forward stroke. Well, on this hole, Larry teed up his ball a little too low and then proceeded to hit the very top of the ball. It is hard to say exactly what happened next, but it would suffice to tell you that the movement of the ball created by his forward swing was minimal compared to the force exerted by his second back swing. It was a solid stroke that resulted in the ball landing ten yards behind him midway between the two tee boxes, nestled under a cactus near a cute little ground squirrel who was as startled as we were.

The local rules allow stroke and distance, requiring you to drop the ball on the line where it entered the desert, no closer to the hole. With this being the case, Larry had to drop the ball on the back tee box for a net loss of 20 yards on his drive! We told him he could just re-tee, but he needed to prove something. We thanked him for entertaining us, but he just grimaced and shook his head in disbelief. Without saying a word, he trudged through the twenty yards of desert, using his driver to knock his ball out from under the cactus on his way to the championship tees. He was careful not to come too close to the cactus for fear of being attacked.

**Don't believe in attacking cactus?
Keep reading.**

Perfection

Most hackers will have the "round of their life" several times during their playing years without ever perfecting even one aspect of their game. Typically, a great drive will be followed by a sliced approach shot. A nice lay-up will be followed by a skulled chip. Ten perfect drives on the range will always result in a topped drive on the first tee. And if you announce to your playing partners that you can read the greens like the back of your hand, you'll be punished on the next hole with a three putt from ten feet.

However, a great majority of hackers will perfect their own unique outburst of exasperation. As you can imagine, few of these personality defining comments would impress your mother. Courtesy of my past playing partners, I will mention only a few of my favorites.

Bob: "Your sister's ass!"

How my sister's ass can possibly influence Bob's swing path is a real mystery. And, besides, Bob's never even met my sister. But when he utters this phrase, it's best if you just nod as if what he said makes perfect sense.

Bill: "Just once, just once, I want to sink a putt!"

Know anybody who has ever said this? Bill used to say this after missing every putt. I cured him of this habit when I once asked him, "If you never once sunk a putt, would you really continue playing this game"?

Joe: "This club is terrible!"

It must be the apparatus. It couldn't possibly be the person swinging the club. But, even so, let us assume that the club is poorly made or the shaft is bent or the head was welded on backwards – why Joe, why are you still using it?

Mike: "I absolutely suck at this game!"

It's a fairly common complaint that I am often been accused of muttering. Since it is usually true, it requires no comment from anyone within response range.

Tee shots always provide the most humor, partly due to the fact that for a true hacker - direction and distance are as predictable as the stock market. It is on the tee box that the following are heard pretty much every single round:

"You have to be kidding me, I never slice my drive!"

"Look at that crap; you know I never hook my drive!"

"Where did that come from? I've never topped my drive before!"

"100 perfect drives on the range and now this! I never miss the ball!"

**To those misguided optimists,
we can all say – "oh yeah…you have".**

Putters Beware

The course can be a dangerous place. Skulled shots that nearly miss a playing partner happen with regularity. Errant drives that threaten the lives of foursomes on neighboring holes are obvious inherent hazards of the game. I have seen the Ranger pelted and ferociously struck balls bouncing around the beer cart as if they were in a pinball machine. However, my favorite is the slice inspired by Satan himself. I'm figuring he has a hand in these because the shot is always followed by someone saying, "What in the hell was that?"

Even the range can be treacherous. Have you seen the movie "Tin Cup?" A silly question for you true hackers! Remember Kevin Costner shanking the ball on a 90-degree angle down the line of professional golfers? I'm sure there are many of us who claim to be the real character behind the one portrayed by Mr. Costner, at least when it comes to mastering the shank. How about those brilliant individuals who absolutely need to retrieve a dribbler hit from the practice mat? I've seen them venture out ten or twelve feet ducking and moving like a medic trying to get to a wounded soldier. And then there was Russ, rest his soul, who gave himself a black eye after a ball he hit ricocheted off the wooden divider that separated his stall from the adjacent one.

But alas, there is the putting green. A refuge from the dangers encountered on the course. What could be safer than the practice putting green? On this patch of solitude, we can relax, reflect and develop a game plan for conquering the course. Sure, there is the occasional ten-foot alligator sunning himself on the warm, soft surface. But that's commonplace for hackers who play golf in Florida. When approached, these beasts almost always quietly saunter off back into the water. Well, almost always. I suppose it can be frightening witnessing this for the first time, but just remember your 2-iron. It's almost impossible to hit a golf ball with it, but it might come in handy against a 300 pound charging reptile.

If you are looking for some real excitement on the green, you need to travel northwest from the Florida everglades to the bayous of Louisiana. It was there that I met up with my friend Shoeless Ed and his cousin Butch. Ed was born and raised in New York City and Butch was a local boy, raised on crawfish and some kind of liquid that can best be described as a combination of jet rocket fuel and Drano.

We had about twenty minutes to kill before our tee time, so Shoeless Ed and I were engaged in a nickel a putt contest. While concentrating on a twenty-footer, a flock of duck flew overhead. They were very low and extremely loud. Now, I know what you're thinking. You're thinking that Shoeless Ed and I were bombarded with duck poop. Well...the first flock flew by without incident or excrement. A minute or two later, a second flock flew towards us. This flock was much larger and noisier. While Ed and I looked skyward in gosh gee wiz city boy fascination, Butch calmly pulled a shotgun out of his golf bag and blasted away! He wasn't a very good shot; something he would prove again and again while playing golf, so a few stray feathers were all we were pelted with.

I was afraid to comment, fearing that Butch would offer me another sip of his wretched toxic cocktail, so I just smiled and went back to putting. I did, however, glance at Ed searching for an explanation. He sensed my fear and quickly dismissed my concern by reminding me that he did warn me about golf being played just a little differently in Louisiana!

**Golf is golf, unless it's
not and then it's not worth playing!**

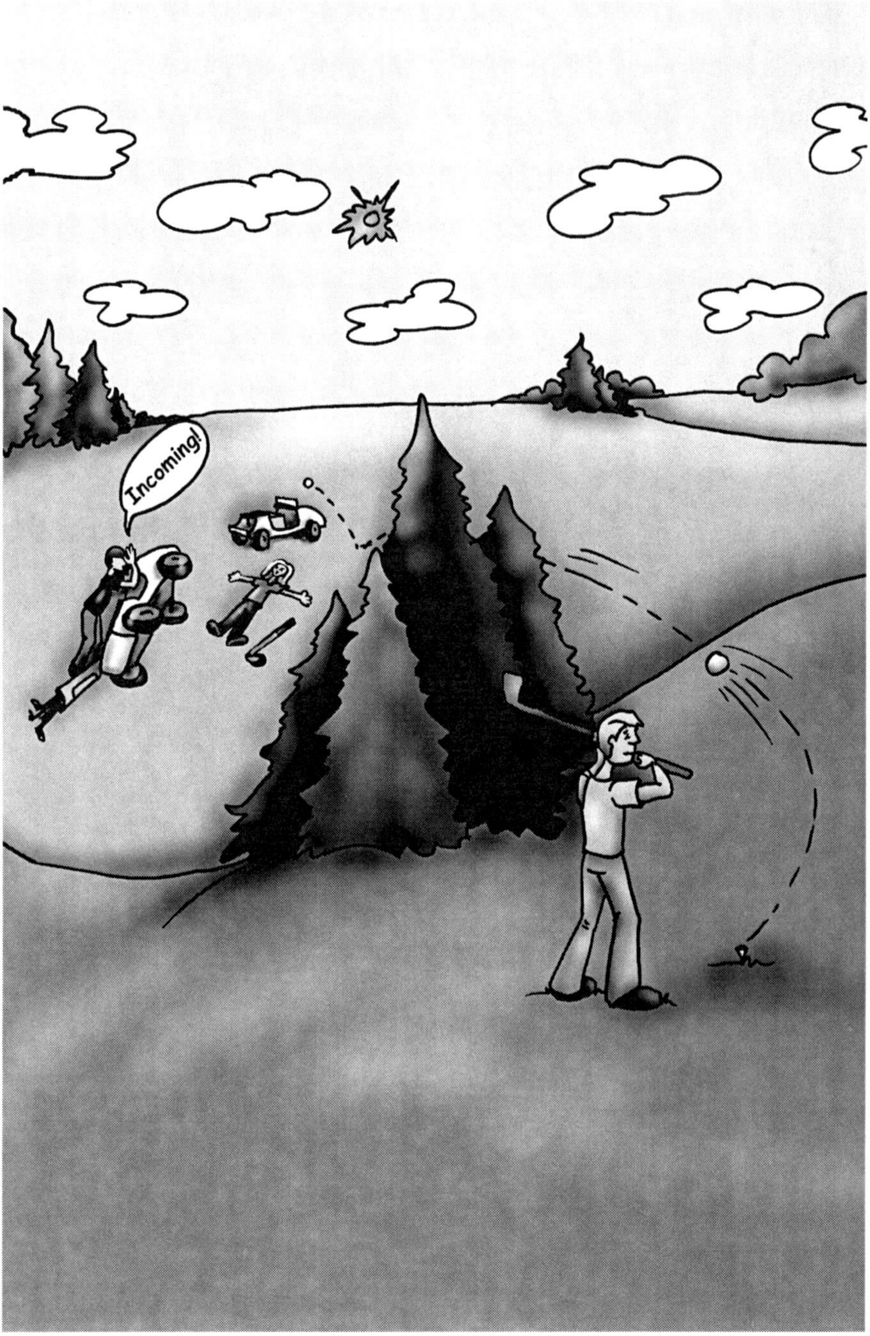
Incoming!

Scramble and the Hedge

Company golf outings, for the uninitiated, can be extremely scary and potentially career damaging. While a member of corporate America, I attended a three-day management conference. The entire first day was devoted to planning for the "Team-Building" event that would take place the afternoon of the second day. Every attendee had to submit their golf handicap to the event coordinator. If you were new to the game of golf but could correctly identify a club out of a line-up of sports equipment, you were granted a not-so generous handicap of 30. If you failed to identify the golf club after three tries, you were given a handicap of 36, the agreed upon maximum strokes allowed. Every player was listed in handicap numerical order starting with the best golfers and ending with those who foolishly thought they could just make a nice long walk of it.

After the talent order was established, the group was divided into quarters with the top 25% assigned the letter "A", the next quarter the letter "B", the third grouping were the "C" golfers and the true hackers were placed in the "D" category. Each team would be comprised of one golfer from each letter group. An asterisk was placed next to name of one golfer in each group. The asterisk person was the designated captain and was in charge of turning in the official scorecard for their team.

With a 22.9 handicap, I was not surprised to find myself in the "C" group. But I was shocked to see the asterisk next to my name. Apparently, organization skills and not putting ability were used to select the captains. Looking at the three names listed under mine, I was positive that my team would be the most dysfunctional foursome in the outing. In fact, before we even left the conference room, Joe "I'm the Pro" Jensen immediately usurped my authority by announcing that he "would take care of the team". I gladly yielded.

However, this greatly upset Sam "I should have been the A player" Spade. Our fourth, Nancy "I've never played or had the desire to play before" Neumeyer could care less about the situation.

The format was a scramble. Each player would tee off and the foursome would proceed to argue over whose drive was best. To add more conflict, one drive from each of the four players had to be used on the front and back nine. After deciding whose drive to use, the happy foursome would all hit from where the chosen drive landed. This methodology would continue for each shot played. However, after the drive, there were no caveats as to whose shot had to be used.

We could, for example, use all of Joe's second shots – which, incidentally, is exactly what he thought.

The putting greens resembled a circus act. Joe the Pro insisted that Nancy putt first with the rest of us positioned behind her to watch the speed and roll. Being the shortest, I would kneel, Sam would crouch over me and Joe would stand on his tippy toes behind Sam. With this format, you would think that with four golfers, one would manage a decent shot at each point of the game. You might also think that given a pair of paper wings, a pig really could fly.

After four holes, I was already convinced that we were out of contention for the Team Low Score Award, which would be presented at dinner that evening. However, Joe and Sam knew that a birdie run would put us at the top of the leader's board so we had a little group meeting on the 5th tee. This tee box had a hedge along the left side. The hedge separated the tee area from the cart path. Considering that a slug with a bad back could traverse the course faster than our foursome, this group meeting did not go over well with the foursome who caught up to us while we were mapping out our strategy.

The waiting foursome positioned themselves safely behind the hedge about 15 yards forward of the white tees giving them a view of the fairway. In an attempt to put some distance between us and this other group, "I'm the Pro", exonerating himself of any blame for our slow play, announced that he would just hit a perfect drive and the rest of us could forgo hitting. Or, as it he put it, "waste our time hacking away".

Well, Joe did hit the perfect shot - a perfect line drive that went through the hedge and hit the back of the front cart that was parked behind the hedge. We heard one scream and then a second as the ball bounced back into the front of the second cart. Startled, but not amused, they backed their carts up a few yards only to be greeted by another hedge shot by Sam! This shot was more lofted and clipped the front of the lead cart and bounced harmlessly down the path.

It was now my turn. Fearing that I would also hit a line drive into the cart, or worse into the forehead of one of the occupants, thus ending their round and my career, I used an iron and aimed well to the right. The club selection would allow me to get under the ball, eliminating the possibility of a line drive. Aiming right should put the hedge, and those foolishly parked behind it, out of play.

I took a mighty swing and the loft of the club did its job – a little too well! The ball went straight up in the air, possibly due to the fact that I teed it up high enough to attract several lost mountain climbers. And because my feet were so awkwardly planted, the ball sort of spiraled up above the low cloud cover. As it descended, it drifted to the left and over the hedge where it landed on the roof of the same cart that we already hit twice.

I would imagine that the odds of three consecutive golfers hitting the same object given only one shot apiece is roughly the same as scoring a double eagle, but we managed to accomplish that feat! I am, to this day, slightly disappointed that we could not make it four for four. Hitting from the red tees, Nancy would have had to hit the ball behind her to make this happen and, despite, her tremendous effort to do so - she duffed one about 20 feet making her drive the best of the hole!

The Golf Course - where balls, friends and enemies are easily found and lost.

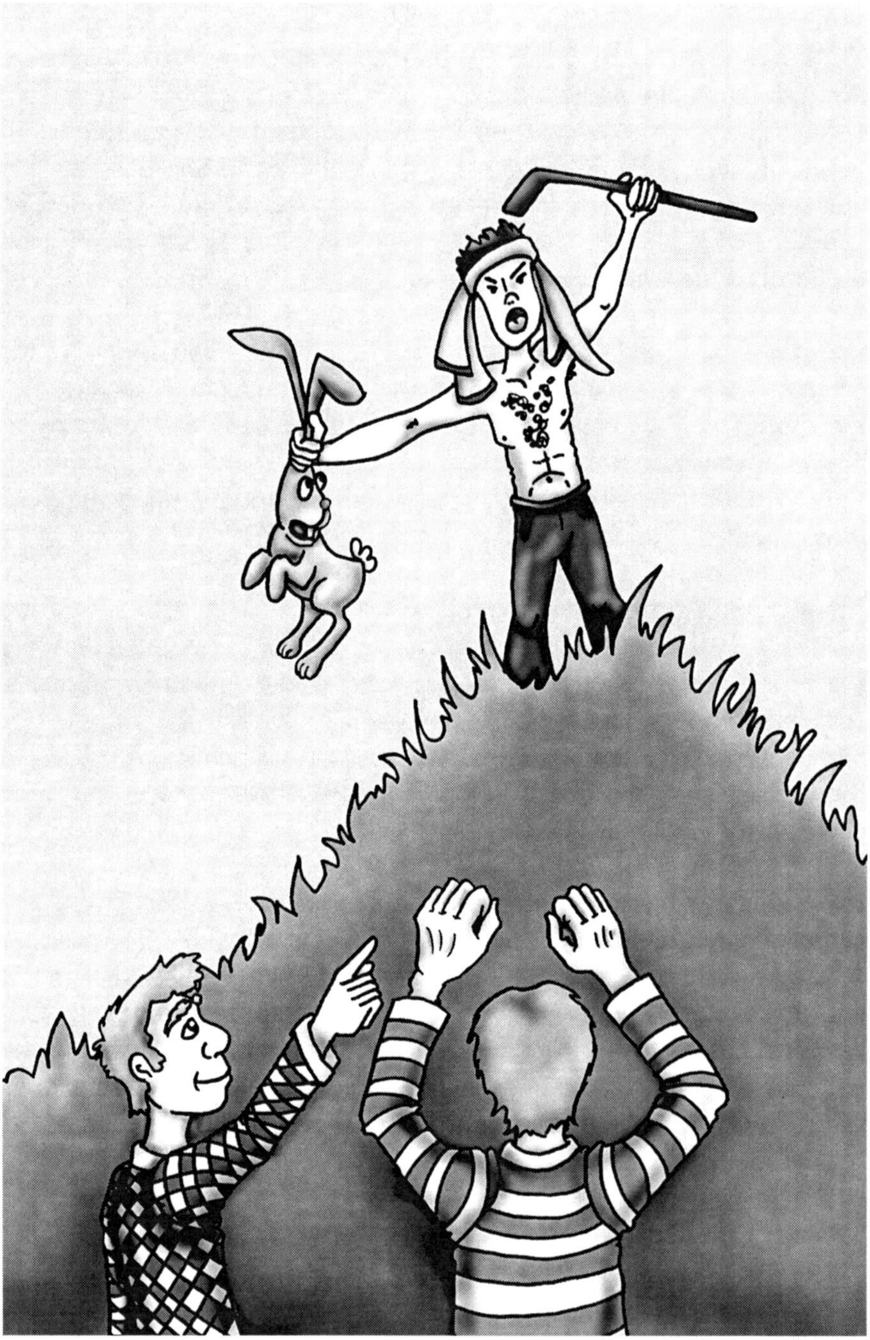

Shoeless Ed Shakes his Head

Have I mentioned that my brother Dom is a doctor? How about that he is a medical pulmonary specialist? And did I also mention that he is a Captain in the U.S. Navy? Did I previously omit the fact that he is an awful golfer?

Well, perhaps comical would be a better description. I invited Doctor Dom to play with me and shoeless Ed for a quick nine. Ed read in some obscure golf magazine that playing bare foot would help achieve the perfect swing. Ed is often seen, in the summer months, arriving at the course in his sandals - which he stows in his golf bag once off the first tee and out of sight of the starter.

The first and I believe last time Shoeless Ed played with Doctor Dom began quite uneventful. It was a sunny pleasant, late afternoon, weekday with a course that was in desperate need of more hackers. In violation of most club policies, the Doctor and I were sharing a bag of clubs. We were also taking our time enjoying the near perfect conditions. Perhaps Ed and I were taking a little too much time. On the third tee, Doctor Dom announced that he needed to get more exercise and that he would play the rest of the round in "speed mode". Not knowing what that was, Eddie and I did not have to wait long to get an answer. Doc teed up his ball, walked back to my bag, grabbed a seven iron and then ran back towards his ball with the club raised parallel to his hips. After striking the ball, as if he were playing polo, he continued to run in the general direction of the severely sliced shot. That's the last we saw of the good doctor for an hour or so.

Sure, we caught glimpses of a shadow in the woods now and then. But it was not until we were on the seventh hole, which lies in a valley, that a confirmed sighting was made. The land slopes up to the highest point on the course two fairways over to the left of where Ed and I stood - me in golf shoes and Ed in his bare feet. The elevation difference between us and the peak of the hill was about 50 feet. This height differential was just enough for movement to catch our eye. When we both turned towards the hill, what we saw may very well remain with us for the rest of our golf playing days. For on that hill was Doctor Dom. His shirt was wrapped around his forehead and both of his hands were raised high above his head. He held my seven iron in his right hand and in his left hand was something we could only guess to be a small, dead, furry woodland creature.

Ed and I continued to play the final holes, meeting up with Doc in the parking lot. His shirt was on and no animal carcasses were in sight. We asked no questions. We received no explanation. It was a perfect ending to another glorious and strange day on the links.

"Golf, like life, is to be enjoyed and not understood."

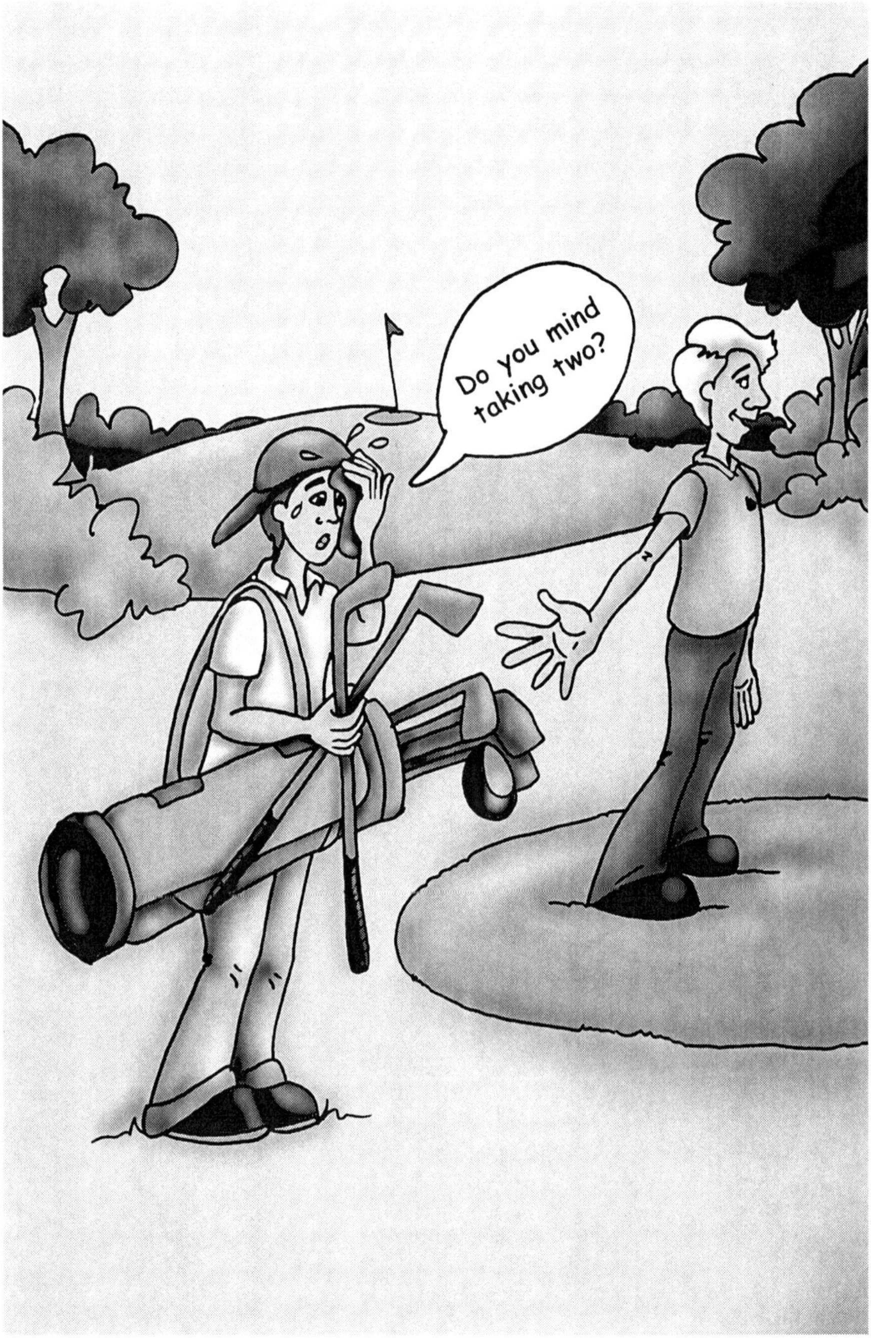
Do you mind taking two?

So, you want to be a Caddy?

Golf caddies are wonderfully knowledgeable individuals who can definitely help lower your score, especially on the putting greens. Their familiarity with the breaks and speed of a rolling ball on each putting surface is often astounding and, if the advice they offer is taken, you putts per hole will almost certainly improve. However, for me, putting was not the challenge I faced. It was the numerous shots I took along the way to the green that caused several of my former playing partners to take up tennis. I often dreamt that using a caddy, talented in proper club selection and possessive of extraordinary patience, would propel me to an envious level of play astounding those fortunate enough to accompany me while I par hole after hole.

When I received a call from Mike, an old High School buddy, inviting me to play at the North Hempstead Golf Course, I was hoping that this could be that day. We were joined by Jim, a mutual friend from our old neighborhood. Although the use of a caddy was not mandatory, it was strongly recommended. To my delight, Mike opted to use them.

Mike had a single digit handicap with a hole in one and a club championship on his golf resume. He was not, what novices affectionately call, a hacker. As for Jim, well…Jim was better than Mike. I had no right playing with them. But since I always provided them with entertaining shots, they enjoyed my company and my money – which always seemed to transfer from my pocket to theirs at the end of every round!

Mike arranged for two caddies. The senior caddy took both his and Jim's bag. The junior caddy carried mine. They handed us our drivers and quickly walked about 200 yards down the left hand-side of the fairway. Mike and Jim hit their drives down the center of the fairway just beyond where the caddies were standing. It was now my turn on the tee box. Hitting a golf ball on a 90 degree angle is extremely difficult. I cannot take credit for achieving this nearly impossible shot, but I came close with a ball that traveled 70 degrees to the right of where I was aiming and into a hedge that separated my tee box from a practice tee. Standing on that practice tee was the Club Pro and two students. Although I startled the three of them, nothing was said.

Meanwhile, my caddy began to move towards me until he was waived off by Mike. Through some elaborate display of long distance hand gestures, Mike indicated to him that I would be hitting another shot from the tee. When my second tee shot followed the same path as the first ball, the Club Pro loudly announced to everyone within a two mile radius, "I've been here for 30 years and have never seen that happen even once!" I wasn't sure if I should feel honored or crawl under the hedge with the two lost balls and remain there until dark. Unfazed, but trying to suppress a laugh, Mike once again waved off the caddy and, displaying a not often seen evil sadistic character flaw, made me hit a third ball from the tee.

Fearing that I would replicate the same shot over and over again until someone grabbed the club from my sweaty grip and bent it over their knee, I aimed well left and dribbled the ball about twenty feet into a sprinkler head cavity next to the left side of the ladies tee box. Not receiving any further guidance from Mike, my caddy jogged back towards me, gently relieving me of my driver and handing me a 4-iron. He also removed my ball from the hole and gave me a nice lie. He then quickly walked about twenty yards down the left hand side of the fairway. At this point, he figured he would not venture too far from me.

Well, as luck would have it, I hit the best 4-iron in my yet undistinguished golf career, smacking it about 200 yards clear across the fairway into the right rough. Off went the caddy, crossing the fairway in pursuit of my long, but errant shot.

I would like to say that I settled down after that disastrous first hole, but I would be lying. Whenever my caddy positioned himself twenty yards from me, I would hit it 200. If he joined the other caddy 200 yards away, I would skull it or shank it or top it – getting 30 yards at best. And never did the ball travel in the direction of where the caddy stood. If he guessed right, it would go way left. If he guessed left, right it would go. I'm pretty sure I even hit one or two shots behind me. And, on more than one occasion, he politely asked if I could take two clubs from him so that he could catch his breath. My guess is that he thought by giving me multiple clubs, he would not have to run back to give me another club when I hit it only halfway to the spot he was hoping I would reach. Feeling a little sympathetic to his plight and seeing that he was clearly winded, I offered to take half the bag.

The highlight of the round definitely occurred on the 13th hole. When it was my turn to tee off, my caddy chose to position himself in the middle of the fairway, about 120 yards away. Since I was yet to hit a ball down the middle, he felt safe there. Since my tee shots ranged from 20 feet to 240 yards, he also figured he would go with the average. Good golfers can get about 100 feet of elevation on their wedge shot. Great golfers can get much higher. I was not using a wedge off the tee, which in retrospect may have been a good idea; however the elevation I achieved was truly impressive! And much to my delight, I also hit the ball straight. While I was admiring the flight path of the ball, my caddy was doing a strange dance. He backed up a few steps and then quickly shuffled to his left, dropped the bag, tripped over it and rolled to his right. The ball landed softly about ten feet from his head. He tried his best to keep his composure for the rest of the round, but he was no match for me. I continued to outwit him at every bend and dog leg on the course!

At the end of the round, the caddy carrying the two bags looked as fresh as when we started. His hair was still combed and he had barely a bead of sweat on his face. By comparison, my caddy looked as if he just wrestled an alligator in a muddy swamp. His hair was disheveled, his shirt tail was hanging out of his pants and you could squeeze a full glass of water from the brim of his hat.

Mike asked me to give my caddy a little extra so that he could dry-clean his grass stained shirt, pants and socks. I immediately obliged while profusely thanking the caddy and telling him that I hope to get another chance to use him in the future. However, that would never happen for a few days later Mike told me that my caddy decided to become the pool lifeguard. It is only a rumor that the fear of encountering me again on the course played a part in his decision to change careers.

Lesson Number Two:
Pity your Caddie.

The Big Miss

As odd as it may seem to the non golfer, the nolfer if you will, it is possible to swing and completely miss the ball. Us hackers know the ball is not moving, no need to remind us. However, we also know that the ability to whiff at the ball increases ten fold for every spectator watching.

So just imagine being at the first tee with a buddy and two acquaintances you've never played golf with before. Now add to the scenario the presence of forty or fifty firemen waiting for their outing to begin. Compound this with the fact that beer was served with breakfast.

The two acquaintances both hit nice drives down the center of the fairway. Now it's your turn. You place your tee in the ground, address the ball, wiggle a little, take a practice swing and then your real swing. You're still looking down, as you should be, and you see the ball still perched atop the tee. It happens, not often - but it does happen. However, imagine if you miss it again and again and again. Imagine the jeers from the firemen – comical and extremely unnerving.

Your buddy, who is yet to tee off, comes forward and gives you the opportunity to compose yourself. He hits a respectable drive and then motions for you to return to the tee. Some friend!

Back you go, insert tee, address the ball, wiggle a little, take a practice swing, and then take your real swing. You're still looking down, like the pro during your last lesson told you to do, and you see the ball glaring back at you like a scorned lover. It's not supposed to happen this often! And the jeers intensify…

"Stand closer to the ball."

"Use a longer club!"

"Take up Tennis!"

"You suck!"

And those were the kind comments. After another a miss or two, who's counting at this point, you finally hit a worm burner 100 yards or so in the general direction of the green. The erupting cheers rival those heard for the final pairing on the 18th green at Augusta.

Sadly, I admit it was I who most probably set a modern day record for the number of consecutive whiffs. I did, however, settle down after carding an eighteen on the 1st hole. I bogeyed the second and then had three consecutive pars. On the sixth tee, George, one of the acquaintances, turned to me, grabbed me by the shoulders and shouted the first words he had spoken since the ceremonial tee toss, "that was the worst case of 1st tee jitters I have ever seen!" And then, in a very civil and friendly tone, he added – "but nice recovery".

In golf, the opportunity for disaster far outweighs the opportunity for good fortune!

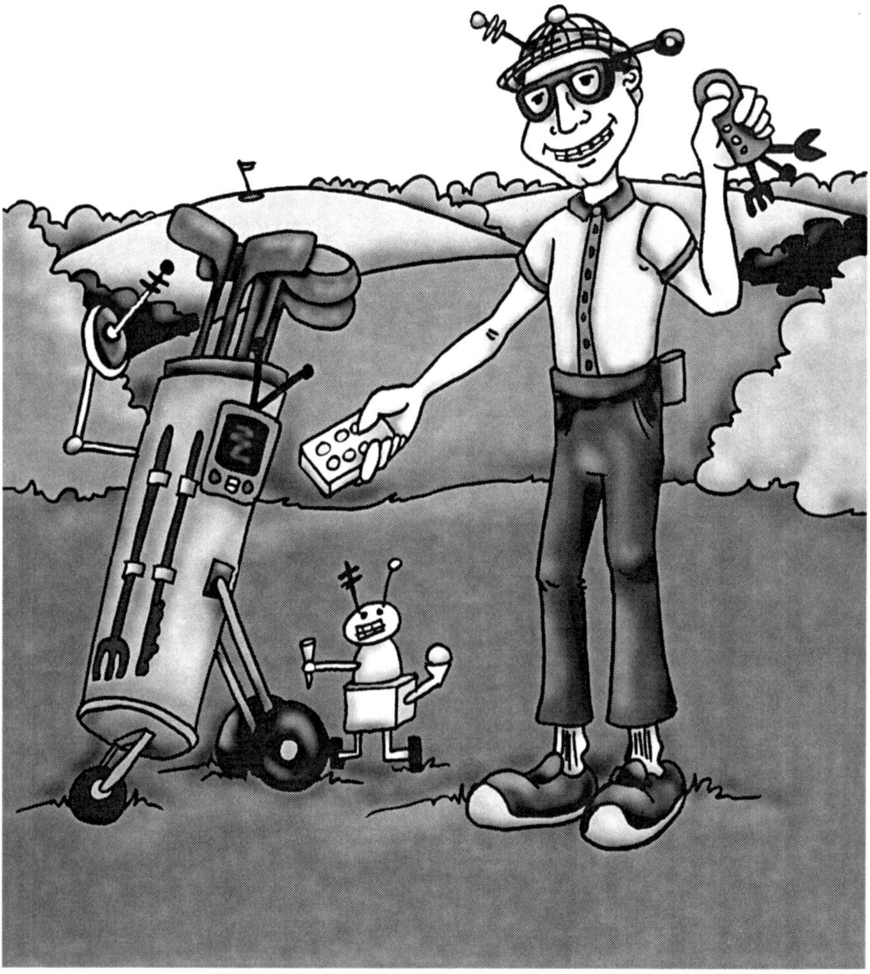

The Gadget Man

Every hacker has at least one device that was purchased because it guarantees to cut five strokes off his score. I've purchased so many of these gadgets that I should be shooting in the twenties.

I've often been compared to Kevin Costner in "Tin Cup" when Renee Russo ventured into his trailer finding him outfitted like a space alien. But nobody, not I, not even Kevin Costner can compare to Gary Medina "engineer extraordinaire". No offense intended, but engineers just do not make good golfers. Their brain chemistry is all off. They can analyze and actually understand all of the facets associated with swing mechanics, but put a club in their hand and you're asking for trouble. Gary was no exception. He spent countless hours experimenting with devices that might correct his truly spectacular slice. He continually modified his equipment, trying to change the weight distribution in his clubs, the ball and his shoes, but nothing could correct his slice. Going to the practice range to work on his swing never entered into this engineer's formula!

His equipment modifications all failed and slowly he came to terms with the fact that he would forever slice. He countered this by aiming approximately 37.5 degrees to the left of the target while swinging. This was scary and not totally effective. His antics never ceased to amaze and frighten his playing partners. Although he aimed left with every drive, his slice would miraculously vanish one out of every 100 attempts – the ensuing damage was often spectacular, but the search and rescue efforts did not sit well with those groups playing behind us. After a near miss with a ten foot square plate glass window and Gary's insistence that we rummage around a homeowner's back and front yard, I encouraged Gary to turn back to science.

I am proud to admit that I was in his foursome when he introduced the "Medina Ball Finder". When Gary placed his ball on the first tee, I noticed a thin gray line around the ball. When I inquired, Gary said - "just watch, or better yet - listen". Gary still aimed 37.5 degrees to the left of the middle of the fairway and he still managed to slice his tee shot into the woods on the right side of the fairway. But he was not at all upset. In fact, he looked very excited and quickly made his way back to the cart where, from his golf bag; he retrieved a small box with several telescoping antennae. He turned a few knobs and the box emitted a low hum.

After the rest of us had hit, we drove off in search of Gary's errant shot. As we neared the spot where we thought we would find the ball, the box hummed much louder. Gary jumped from the cart and approached a ball near the edge of the woods. When he was a few feet away, the hum became an ear splitting screech followed by a mind numbing wail. As neighboring golfers ran for cover, assuming it was either an air raid or a warning that lightning was approaching, we begged him to shut off his contraption.

Gary never did correct his slice, but he lost far fewer balls and his pace of play improved considerably. Last I heard he was outfitting the Medina ball finder with a soundless gauge and needle to indicate when he was closing in on his prey. Like most good engineers, Gary refuses to market his invention until perfection is reached. But, as with his golf swing, that may never be achieved.

The seemingly unattainable is achieved by those with enough desire!

Up, up and ...away?

"It's still raining. Can't you hear it crashing off the roof like machine gun fire?"

"It's barely a drizzle and the weatherman said it would end after midnight."

Staring out the window for the 14th time, my wife finally had enough.

"Get out! Gather up your golf clothes and go sleep on the couch or, better yet, stand outside and watch the rain for the next six hours!"

At 3:00 AM it was still raining and I was pacing my living room and silently cursing the weatherman. From under the couch, my two cats curiously watched my quiet tirade.
I stayed indoors and fell asleep when the rain stopped.

The alarm in the bedroom must have gone off. Either that, or there was an intruder in my bedroom and my wife was swearing that she was going to send him to an early grave.

After a short, too short, fog delay and no threat of rain in the immediate forecast, my foursome was given the green light to tee off. Joe, Mark, Bobby and I were a little hesitant to hit because the visibility was about 50 yards. The starter assured us that the pea soup would burn off in ten or fifteen minutes and since he did not want to back up the course, he insisted we get going. Carts were banned until the fairways firmed up a bit, so even without the fog, keeping on schedule would be a difficult task.

The first three holes were torturous, we might have well have been blindfolded. By the fourth hole, the pea soup did indeed burn off and was replaced by a light chicken noodle. There were periodic breaks of sunlight and visibility was now 75 yards! Joe was almost out of balls, so he was thrilled when he hit a nice drive on a short par four. It was not a long drive, but it was straight and just finding the ball was a minor victory for Joe. Being in unfamiliar territory, the middle of the fairway, Joe was a little nervous when he played his second shot. Mark, Bobby and I took position a few yard behind Joe – all intensely focusing on the ball in hopes that at least one of us would be able to follow its path. Joe took a full swing with a fairway wood and all four of us looked skyward into the murky mist.

"Didn't see it," I said.

"Think it went left," said Bobby.

"Don't think it got too far off the ground," said Mark.

"I hit the snot out of it!" said Joe.

We fanned out and looked. We stumbled upon Bobby's and my second shots and chipped them onto the green. Mark's second shot was irretrievably lost, so we resumed looking for Joe's ball.

We looked left, right, straight, long and short – all to no avail. We suggested dropping a ball, but Joe would not give up. He insisted that we go back to where he hit from and he would "recreate" the shot. We found the exact spot where he took that shot. We know it was the exact spot because the ball was still there. At first we were not sure, but Mark saw a tiny bit of white and after digging a little, Joe's ball plopped out from the mud. His shot traveled a total of 1 ½ inches, straight down into mother earth.

If that is not bizarre enough, two shots later, Joe's wedge shot landed on top of a bush. It was perched like an egg in a nest. It was actually a pretty good lie for a 50 foot giant. He had to smack the ball like a baseball on a three-foot tee. Having been an excellent ball player in college, he hit his best shot of the day!

At the bar, after the round, we debated for hours over which was the better shot - Joe's wedge to hedge play or the disappearing ball trick. Either way, they'll always be fondly remembered by four aging hackers.

**Even a blind squirrel finds
an acorn now and then.**

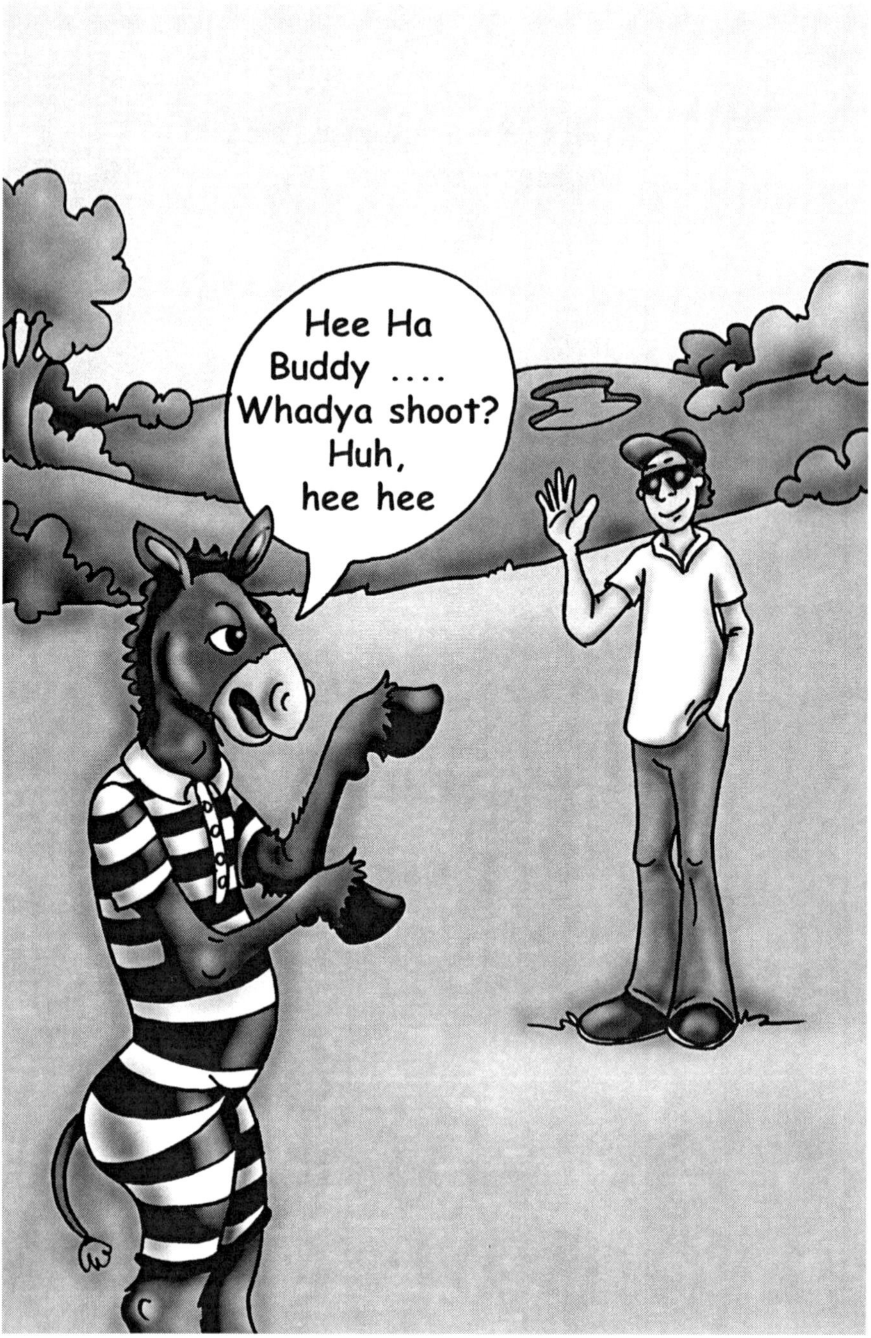
Hee Ha Buddy .... Whadya shoot? Huh, hee hee

"Whadyashoot?"

You've enjoyed a pleasantly frustrating round of golf and you meet up with a buddy later in the day. You're still trying to forget the bunker shot you hit sideways, the four-putt on the 15th and the approach shot on 18 that approached the definition of absurdity. To worsen matters, you haven't played that poorly since you golfed with the smirking demented hyena who is now staring you in the face.

"So, so whadya shoot?"

If you had a club in hand, you would surely whack him and bury his body in the bunker you spent the morning trying to get out of. But, being polite, you tell him "around 90". The fact that you carded a 102 after giving yourself two mulligans and a gimme on the 18th is fine because the truth is you had "around 90" at one point in the round.

So I go to the range for a very rare lesson - true hackers avoid these at all costs. Here is how the lesson went....

Pro: What da ya shoot?

Me: Mid to high 90's.

Pro: Ok, let's see you hit a few seven irons.

I hit five perfect shots. They all land on the green that I am aiming for and the Pro nods his head.

Pro: Not bad.

He hands me my driver and I proceed to hit five consecutive beauties and I'm thinking this guy loves me! I turn to him to receive the words of encouragement I so desperately seek.

Pro: Mid nineties huh? Your putting must really suck.

The truth hurts!

All true hackers dream of a "1" on the scorecard.

My wife had a total of "one" after two holes! Why is it that after you play miniature golf nobody asks "whadyashoot"? My wife was very disappointed that no hyenas were around to ask "Whadyashoot" after she had a total of "one" stroke after two holes of play! She was very proud that her very first putt of the round landed into the cup on the second hole! She was so impressed and excited that she wanted every hyena to know about it. But alas, she had to bring up the topic with everyone she ran into during the following two weeks.

The golf gods certainly do work in mysterious ways!

Who needs friends anyway!

I have some non-golfer friends. These NGFs are still nice people, but they have more than just their one obvious flaw. Take Joey D. for example. Not only is he an NGF, he is also oblivious about my passion for the game. He and his wife, also an NGF, ordered quite a few household furnishings that were delivered via UPS. Amongst the ten boxes that were delivered, were two that did not belong to them. Joey immediately contacted UPS and informed them of the mistake. They assured him that someone would be by to retrieve them.

A few weeks later, Joey placed another call to UPS. Perhaps, thought Joey, someone might be curious as to the whereabouts of the golf clubs they ordered. Ping golf clubs! Anyway, UPS once again told Joe that they would dispatch a driver to pick them up. Months later, Joey stored the two boxes in the back of his garage and soon forgot about them. Do you think he would mention this to me? No! Not once did he mention them to his, very vocal avid hacker, friend.

For three years they sat in a corner, unused, unloved, un-swung until Joey's wife decided to clean the garage. They agreed to place a classified ad in a local rag.

Two sets of Ping Golf Clubs.
Never used.
$150

The circulation of this particular newspaper was about 5000. Of those 5000 households, one can safely assume that 15% contain one or more hackers. Of those hacker households, clearly 99% of them would gladly pay $150 for two sets of ping clubs. The last 1% would hold off for a better deal. So it is no surprise that Joey D. received 749 telephone calls within hours of placing the ad. Of course, being an NGF, he did not understand why. So, at this point, Joey called me. Right? No! It was not until the day after the luckiest hacker in the world parted with a measly $150 for two sets of clubs that Joey opened his mouth to me! Did I mention they were Ping?

The NGF – you can love them, but can you ever truly understand them?

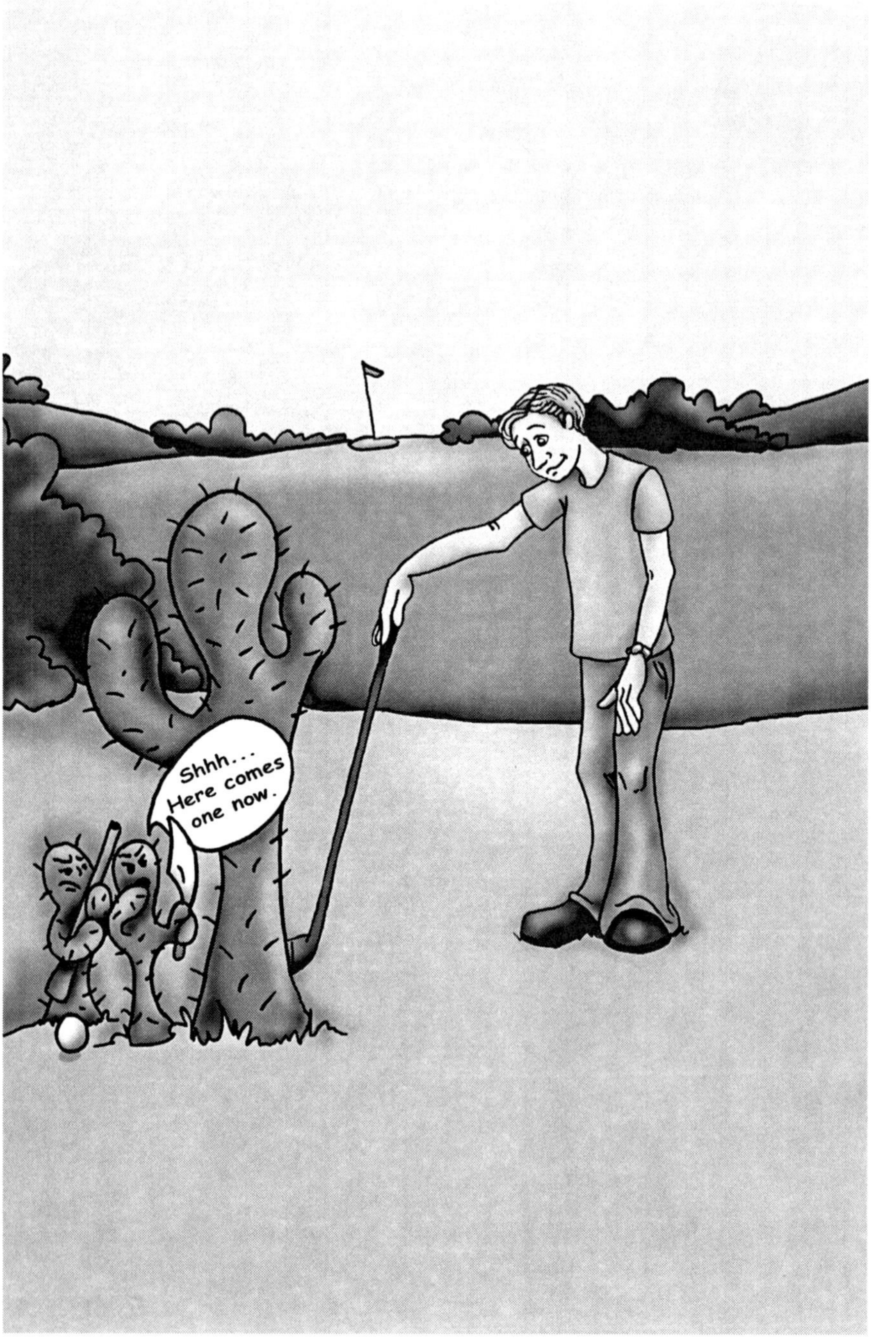
Shhh... Here comes one now.

Wildlife

Sure, we have all tangled with the alligator that refused to budge from his sun spot on a Florida green. And then there are the omnipresent Canadian geese. They'll move a little when you walk toward them, but trying to shape your tee shot around the flock sitting in the middle of the fairway could present itself as a real challenge. Turtles, possums, squirrels, bees, ticks, hornets - all commonplace. And fauna? A case of poison ivy, poison oak, or poison sumac are not even worthy of mention. However, what about the most dangerous adversary Mother Nature places in the path of the true hacker? Single digit handicappers need not know about this crafty nuisance, since it is not found on the fairway or any other place the ball is intended to land. You must venture off into the Arizona wilderness to encounter this creature. I'm referring to, of course, the jumping cholla.

In Arizona, many courses offer very nice amenities, such as a greeter. The greeter meets you at the first tee to explain some of the challenges the course has to offer as well as some of the rules peculiar to their course. "Watch out for the jumping cactus," said our greeter, a very pleasant woman well into the back nine of her life. She even pointed one out. A fairly harmless looking plant with what is best described as pickles protruding from the main stem. She told us that they can sense body heat and to protect itself, can shoot its needles a foot or more.

Were we skeptical? Absolutely!

Were we afraid? Absolutely not!

"Now, if one attacks you", she said", you must remove the spines with two of your irons. Hold one steady on each side of the spines, like giant tweezers, and pull."

Were we laughing? What do you think?

So off we went, assuming that our new friend spent a little too much time in the sun without a hat.

I believe it was the seventh hole that Bobby hit his tee shot off the fairway. To be perfectly honest, he hit pretty much all of his tee shots off the fairway - but this particular one landed a good 50 yards squarely in the middle of desert. We heard the scream, but it was not one of pain - but more of disbelief. Perhaps because Bobby kept shouting, "I can't believe this. I can't believe this! Look at this unbelievable shit!"

Our wrinkled protector warned us about the attacking cactus, but when she said the spines shoot from the cactus, we expected the skinny needles to shoot. So we all chanted "Bobby's being a baby", until we saw him emerge from the desert with a six-inch green thorny plump dill pickle sticking straight out of his leg just below where his shorts ended! And not a hamburger sized slice, but the whole friggin pickle!

We immediately went to work. I yelled, "John, grab your 3 and 4 iron." "No way", he says, "use your own clubs; I'm not getting Bobby's blood on my new clubs!" "Ok, Tommy - can you grab some." "Sure," he says as he pulls two clubs from **my** bag. On the fourth attempt, the tweezers method worked and all that remained was a twenty-four-hour rash and a good story to tell our buddies back home!

Danger lurks
where least expected.

Wolf

Never underestimate the power of a wager. I've seen single digit handicappers fold like cheap umbrellas when faced with having to sink a three-footer on the 18th to win a $2 bet.

Silence is expected when a player is taking a swing. In my regular foursome, heckling, badgering and being downright nasty are acceptable between shots.

Skins, match play and best ball cart golf are all easily explainable and very popular golf wagers. But my group prefers the almost inexplicable game of "wolf". To begin, as with most rounds, a tee is tossed skyward and the player to whom it points is designated player #1. However, in "wolf" this player does not have to tee off first. The tee is tossed again to determine player #2 and once more for player #3. The remaining player, of course, becomes #4.

Player #1 then decides if he wants to tee off first, second, third or fourth. Golfer #2 gets his choice of the remaining three spots and the #3 selects from the remaining two. Golfer #4 is told when it's his turn to play.

The order that has now been established will remain constant throughout the round, however it will shift one player each and every hole. On the second tee, whoever started on the first hole would go second, the second from the first tee would go third, the third from the first would go fourth and the fourth from the first would go…well, first, of course. Confusing yet? Well, let's go back to the first tee and try to clear things up.

After the first golfer on the first tee, who may or may not have been player #1 for reasons that will become obvious by the time you finish reading this story, hits his first shot, the player who is teeing up 4th decides if he wants to take the 1st golfer as his partner for the 1st hole. If he does not desire to do so, he says "pass". He does this again after the second and third golfers hit their shot. If he selected a playing partner for the hole, the format is low total gross. So, for example, if he selects the player who teed off third, his score and that of this player will be added and then compared to the total score of the other two players. Whichever pair has the lowest score wins the hole.

To keep track of the wager, a separate card is recommended. On this card, the two winning golfers for hole #1 would get a "1" for that hole while the two losing golfers would get a "-1".

Clear yet? Well, let's go back to the first tee one last time. If the player who teed up 4th is not impressed, by the tee shots of the other three members in his foursome, he can opt to be the "lone wolf" for the hole. If his score for the hole is better than that of any of the other three players, he wins the hole and, on the separate scorecard, records a "3" for that hole. All of the other players card a "-1". If the "lone wolf" ties with one or more of his fellow golfers for low score, all four players get a "0" for the hole and the next hole is worth double! If the "lone wolf" loses to one or more of the other three golfers, he gets a "-3" and the other players all get a "1".

Since the player rotation changes each hole, all players will be the wolf either four or five times and thus the reason why the tee tossing is not taken lightly! At the end of the round, the score for each hole is tallied by player. A positive number means that you have won something and a negative number means that you have lost something. The final score for each player, when added together, should equal zero so that there is an equal number of something won and something lost. The something could be nickels, dollars, beers, chicken wings or Ferraris. This must be decided before the tossing of the tee.

Of course, and this is why we often bring our accountant along, there can be side bets. Greenies, sand saves and birdies are all cause for adding and subtracting nickels or Ferraris from each hole.

But sometimes, it is the impromptu side bet that is the most fun. Like on the 12th green at the Hannah golf course in Margaretville, NY. On that hole, I opted to be the "lone wolf" after all three of my playing partners hit their drives out of bounds! I thought, "This should be a cinch to capture 3 chicken wings!" I responded to their failure with a great drive and an even better approach shot. I was on the green in two and only three feet from the pin! With a birdie, I could add yet another chicken wing to my score. Now, I must tell you that the slope between my ball and the cup was severe. The fact that the ball did not roll closer to the hole on its own accord was, and will always remain to be, mystifying. Whoever decided to place the flagstick on this slope with the stick making a 75 degree angle with the ground, must have been an evil man!

All three of my playing partners recovered nicely and found themselves on the green below the pin – a much more preferable position than my ball. Bobby and Tommy both two-putted and carded sixes. Johnny holed his first putt for a five. I could make the birdie and get four beers for my effort. But it was also nice to know that I could two-putt from three feet and still pick up three! I lined it up, twice, got my feet set, took a practice putt and was all ready to execute a perfect pendulum swing when Johnny yelled, "double or nothing"!

"For the birdie," I replied.

"No," he said, "for the hole."

"I'd have to three-putt to tie you," I replied with a look that said "you have a cucumber growing out of your right nostril".

I could not imagine 3-putting from three feet, so I stammered, "You're, you're, you're on!"

With my adrenaline soaring, I knocked my first putt well past the hole, down the slope and off the green. Fearing that my second putt would fall short and roll back to where I now stood, I hit it too hard and it landed roughly where I began my first putt. Having had some experience now with this downhill tap, I hit it softly and it rolled right towards the center of the hole. As if an invisible wall was temporarily erected an inch from the hole, the ball abruptly stopped rolling. Well, I did not birdie the hole and did not pick up four Ferraris; I also did not two-putt for three beers. In retrospect, I would have been satisfied with a three-putt and a "0" for the hole. But, I four-putted. I four-putted the 12th at Hannah from three feet away!

This happened in 1996 and since then, whenever one of us who witnessed this colossal collapse makes a mess of a good situation on the golf course or anywhere else on planet earth, we call that mess a "Hannah 12".

To the Victor, the spoils.
As for the rest of us, we'll pick up the tab.